PISTOL PETE
MARAVICH

THE MAKING OF A BASKETBALL SUPERSTAR
PISTOL PETE MARAVICH
BY BILL GUTMAN

GROSSET & DUNLAP
A National General Company
Publishers   New York

COPYRIGHT © 1972 BY BILL GUTMAN

LIBRARY OF CONGRESS CATALOG CARD NUMBER: 78-184925
ISBN: 0-448-01973-6

ALL RIGHTS RESERVED
PUBLISHED SIMULTANEOUSLY IN CANADA

PRINTED IN THE UNITED STATES OF AMERICA

For Beth

Acknowledgments

The author would like to thank the following people for their help in supplying valuable background material for this book:

George Cunningham, *Atlanta Constitution;* Nick Curran of the National Basketball Association; Peter Finney, *New Orleans States-Item;* Paul Phillips, North Carolina Department of Conservation and Development; Bob Bradley, Clemson College Sports Information Director; Frank Weedon, North Carolina State Sports Information Director; Bud Johnson, Louisiana State University Sports Information Director; Paul Manasseh, Louisiana State University; Tom McCollister, Atlanta Hawks Publicity Director; Walt Hazzard, John Valley and Richie Guerin of the Atlanta Hawks; Ed McClean and Olin Broadway, Jr., coaches from Needham-Broughton High; Ed Biedenbach, Tom Mattocks, Jeff Tribett and Rich Hickman; Al Silverman, *Sport* Magazine. And special thanks to Press Maravich for his time, cooperation and willingness to talk about a sport he loves.

Contents

Prologue	11
Chapter I	13
Chapter II	55
Chapter III	125
Statistics	187

PISTOL PETE MARAVICH

Prologue

He speeds over the court in easy loping strides, the basketball moving like a yoyo off his fingertips. In a game of bursts and screeches, he displays the grace of a dancer, a silkiness of motion that has no equal. In a world where even storklike sevenfooters are acrobats, this kid remains special. When Pete Maravich has the ball, the whole bag of magic is possible.

Years before, when he was a collegian in the Bayou country of Louisiana, even then he made grown men marvel. A black coach at an all-black high school once saw Maravich spin and soar through move after move and promptly exclaimed, "My God, he's one of us."

In fact, though, Maravich is one of a kind—a lean and loose wizard of the funky and unbelievable. Now as a pro for the Atlanta Hawks, he is no less to behold. In the Alexander Memorial Coliseum, or in any other pro arena, Maravich turns the night around when he plays. Whirling through and around the most cunning players in the world, he creates shots that sometimes defy the eloquence of the team's announcer, Skip Caray, or the writers who travel with the team.

What Maravich can do with a basketball places him outside the usual experience of pro basketball fans. His game is seductive, and he knows it. And the pride he takes in stretching his game to its limits is what captivates people. It expresses to them, as never before, the many-splendored game of basketball.

Chapter 1

Aliquippa, Pennsylvania, is one of the many tough steel towns on the rim of the Greater Pittsburgh area.

On a bright and sunny June afternoon there in 1948, Press Maravich turned to Doctor H.B. Jones and said he wanted a boy.

"Make it a boy," he snapped, "and I pay, but if it's a girl, you pick up the tab. How about it?"

Dr. Jones must have known something.

"You're on," he said.

Later that day the doctor walked directly into the delivery room of the nearby Sewickley, Pennsylvania, hospital, and covered his wager. Emerging from the room hours later, he looked at his friend Press with a wry smile and announced, "You pay."

And so was the entry of Peter Press Maravich heralded into the world.

A boy for Papa Press. And, who knows, maybe a ballplayer.

Only Press would have thought so. A man for whom basketball was his life's blood, he swears that he saw signs of the kid's calling even in the cradle. "As an infant he already had instinctive ability. You could see it in the way he reacted to the things around him. The toys in his crib, the things he played with around the house. To tell you the truth, I think he was born with basketball in his genes."

As a matter of fact, many people thought the same of Press. In Logstown, not far from Aliquippa, Pennsylvania, he had taken to a game that was completely alien to the immigrant Maraviches, who eked out their existence in places like Kidd Drawn Steel, the Vulcan Crucible Steel, Jones & Loughlin. For the many Serbians and Yugoslavs who settled there, the mills were the only way to make a living. Press' dad and uncles worked there. Their life was relatively uncomplicated, their tastes simple. Most of them thought that their children would follow them into the mills after high school. Some did. The ones who didn't discovered a way out.

For Press Maravich, it was basketball. "We used to play ball on the street corner," he recalls. "Our hoop was any kind of box or basket that we could hook up on a pole. And the ball . . . what a concoction that was. We started with an empty can, then put a stone in it for weight. Next we stuffed and wrapped it in newspaper, and finally tied it all together with that black, electrical tape. Naturally, the ball didn't have much bounce and that limited us. But we still played a hard, fast game. There was a lot of crisp passing and cutting, and quick, short shots. We played every night by the street light until the cops came and chased us away."

Few men in the town took any real interest in the strange game the boys played. One who did was a local clergyman known as Preacher Anderson. He saw the boys' plight and sought to do something about it. The Preacher soon had two real baskets rigged up in his church, and the boys had a chance to play indoors. There was only one hitch—Preacher Anderson would let them play basketball only if they attended his Sunday School.

"We all agreed to go to classes," says Press. "They lasted for an hour and then we got to play ball. I must have been about nine or ten at the time. Anyway, we played for hours on end every day. And I never missed a Bible class. I quickly became very interested in what Preacher Anderson had to say. I've never forgotten any of it and I still read my Bible faithfully today. As for basketball, that was just a case of love at first sight. I guess I was sort of born with the game in me, too. And the church was the only place to play. We kept at it there right into junior high school."

Press and his friends needed real dedication to keep playing, because there was no encouragement at home. "My father was a big man," he recalls, "maybe 250 pounds. His three cousins were the same way. We called them 'the four tons.' Anyway, they all loved music. Some nights they'd come home from the mills together, have dinner, then just sit around drinking wine and singing songs from the old country until they got tired and went to bed.

"One day, one of those traveling salesmen came around with a banjo. He played it for my father and his cousins, some traditional southern songs, I think. I remember my father really falling in love with the instrument. The guy had some kind of deal where you take lessons for one dollar per week and at the end of the year get to keep the banjo. Like most parents, my father wanted me to take music lessons. I thought it was the most sissyish thing in the world, but he made me do it for six months. Then another guy came around with the same deal on a violin. And wouldn't you know it, for the next year I was taking violin lessons."

But Press weathered the musical storm and continued playing basketball. With long, persistent practice, he made his high school team in the eighth grade and was a starter right through to graduation. It wasn't easy. He had to work in the steel mills from midnight to 8 A.M., then find time for his studies, for basketball, and for a little sleep.

"It's a funny thing," he says, "with all that other stuff—the banjo and violin lessons, and having to work all night in the mills—there was never any thought of giving up basketball. That was in me to stay. We certainly weren't students of the game by any means, but I was already attracted by all the individual skills and fundamentals there were to master. And you have to play the game by instinct. You couldn't think. You had to react like an animal out there." Still, Press's routine wasn't that unusual, especially for a kid who had interests other than the mills. Working always came first. His father saw to that. Anything else had to be squeezed in, with sleep the likely victim. All the kids who aspired to lives other than in the mills had to fight on their own from the beginning.

The familial support that Press lacked as a youngster was certainly not a problem for Pete though. Press didn't follow Doctor Spock or any other authority in priming his son. When Pete could barely walk, Press began rolling a rubber ball to him along the floor of their Aliquippa home. It became a regulation basketball when Pete was about three—old enough not to fall over like a bowling pin when it came at him.

Press waited until the boy was six before making the big move. He set up a hoop in the backyard and urged his son to play. Pete blithely ignored him. "I got him his own ball for Christmas," says Press, "but he wouldn't even look at it. My wife began telling me not to worry, that maybe he'd be a trumpet player. But I couldn't help wondering when he'd pay some attention to the ball.

"Then one afternoon I was taking some shots. He was watching me with those big eyes of his. I hit a bunch of shots in a row and I guess he thought it was easy. So he finally came over, cocky, just like he is now, picked up the ball and took a shot. Well, he missed, and maybe it's lucky he did. Because he got mad, and when he got mad I knew I had him hooked."

Not entirely. Pete still found time for other games. "Like most kids his age," Press says, "he changed with the seasons. In the fall it was football, then basketball in the winter, and baseball as soon as the good spring weather came in. I remember when he was seven or eight he announced he was going to be a baseball player. That lasted a few months. Then he announced he was going to be a great quarterback. That's how it went."

Even then Press felt that to be a great player, a boy had to practice all year round. "I still don't believe a boy can play three or four sports in high school and really excel at one of them. But it applies to basketball more so than the others. A kid really has to concentrate."

Press kept after Pete in those early years, but without much success. As soon as the papers began to carry stories of spring training in Florida, Pete wanted to play baseball. That would precipitate the usual argument, with Press telling his son to stick with basketball and Pete putting the linseed oil on his fielder's mitt. On one beautiful spring day, when Pete was about nine, he was again starting to yearn for baseball. On the verge of tears, a bat on his shoulder, a glove in his hand, he begged his father to play ball with him.

"I always knew just how far I could take him," says Press. "So I figured it was time to feed his appetite. We went out onto a field near our home. The sun was bright and directly over our heads. I began hitting him some fungoes, trying to get the ball as high as I could. Well, he was running back and forth, catching the ball, a big smile on his face. Then it happened. He misjudged one or lost it in the sun. Anyhow, it hit him smack on the forehead. He started crying and by the time we got home had a welt on his head the size of an egg.

"I stayed up with him all night, putting ice on his head and talking to him. And you know what? Neither one of us ever mentioned baseball again. But the funny thing is, I think he could have been a really good baseball player. He had that animal instinct there, too. But don't get me wrong. I'm not complaining."

"From then on," Pete confirms, "I played basketball something like forty-seven weeks of the year. During the summer I was out on the court at eight in the morning and played until it got dark. When we moved to Clemson, South Carolina, I used to open the Y.M.C.A. and play till they kicked me out."

Even then, Pete had a feeling for the game other kids didn't. As a college coach, Press took him into the locker rooms whenever his squads played. The sights and sounds of the game became ingrained in Pete. He watched the players dress, heard their talk and was privy to both the good and bad times.

Still, Papa Press knew that kids were fickle about their games. So he schemed to keep his boy's interest in basketball. "I had to start early and keep working on him all the time," confesses Press. "Sometimes I'd go out in the back yard and start shooting. When I knew Pete was watching me I'd go into my act."

The act consisted of a variety of trick shots—behind-the-back, over-the-head, or bounced into the hoop. "I really made like I was enjoying myself, like I was having the time of my life. And I could see he was going for it."

When Pete was about nine, Press had begun challenging him to games of "horse" at their backyard hoop. They were quite a sight—the crewcut, leathery-faced father and the thin, wide-eyed youngster, throwing shots, grinning, teasing, hollering. "We had a heck of a time," says Press. "I'd encourage Pete to take different kinds of shots and really make a fuss when he made one. A lot of the times I'd let him win and pretend I was really angry. I wanted him to know that I didn't like to lose."

Press Maravich was on the road to building a basketball player, but he knew that ultimately it would be up to Pete. In the meantime, he left nothing to chance.

"Pete was always a small kid. He didn't really mature physically until he entered college," says Press. "Once he started playing a lot of ball, he began worrying about growing. All kids think of basketball players as pretty tall guys. I'm just a shade over six feet and my wife is about 5-8, but Pete still worried about hitting that six-foot mark. One night he said to me, 'Dad, I'll never make a basketball player if I don't grow some more.' I could tell he was down on himself, really worried about it. So I told him if he would hang from the door frame for ten minutes a night he'd start growing. Well, the kid did this every night, religiously. And wouldn't you know it, soon after that he started growing like a goony bird.

"But don't get me wrong. I don't want every kid in America going around hanging from the door frames. Pete was just about ready to grow anyway. I was just lucky to hit on it at the right time."

The coach always seemed to know best when it came to his son. "I knew I had to get Pete to perfect the fundamentals," says Press. "But fundamentals can be dull. I learned to watch his face. That was the indicator. For instance, if he was practicing the chest pass, I'd wait until that bored look started creeping onto his face. Then I'd make him switch to, say, a one-handed pass. I'd watch him again. When he started looking bored, I'd say let's try something different. So we'd go to a behind-the-back pass. It excited Pete, kept his interest, and he practiced it as hard and long as anything else. Now he throws that kind of pass maybe 50 feet with the same accuracy of someone else throwing a regular pass."

There were drills, too, serving to improve Pete's ball

handling. He developed these to such a degree that they became a show in themselves. Even spinning a basketball was a singular routine.

"The first thing I learned to do was spin the basketball on my fingertips," says Pete. "I'd start with my index finger, then go down my hand, spinning the ball on each finger. I do a quick change in one variation where it looks like I'm spinning it on all five fingers at once. When I started spinning, I'd spin the ball for as long as anybody wanted me to. I'd make bets on how long. I had it spinning one time for about 50 minutes straight. I had a full nail, a half-inch nail, all worn down, and the whole thing was bleeding.

"Now I can spin the ball down under my arm, go inside out and come all the way around, keeping it going. Outside-in is even harder. Another variation is spinning the ball, then flicking it behind my back and catching it on one finger, still maintaining the spin. I used to use this drill in our team warmups before games, just to get loose."

As time went on, the drills increased in number. Most of them were devised by Press—sometimes in his sleep. "When that happened, I'd just write the idea down, show it to Pete the next day, and we'd give it a name." The names were almost as intriguing as the drills—the "ricochet," the "bullet ricochet," the "pretzel," the "walking pretzel" and "dribbling pretzel," the "seesaw" drill, the "punching bag" drill. Nobody in the game ever had so stunning a training program, and Pete performed his drills on into the pros.

The "pretzel" was a hand-reaction drill. Pete placed his left hand behind his left leg and his right hand in front of and between his legs, leaning as he did. He'd hold the ball with his right hand, and the object was to change hands with the ball, moving his hands in a figure-eight fashion around his legs. He'd go back and forth with the ball as fast as he could. The trick was to keep the ball stationary, keep it in place in front of his body and between his legs. He could do this faster than the eye could see.

For the "ricochet" Pete stood with his feet spread shoulder-width apart. He took the ball with both hands and threw it between his legs at a 45 degree angle, catching it behind his back. Then he threw it from back to front the same way, going back and forth continually.

In the variation called the "bullet ricochet," he slammed the ball as hard as he could from way above his head and tried to catch it behind him. "You really can't see my hands move on this one," he once said, "they're going so fast. People have sat there and said, honestly, truthfully, that they had no vision of my hands moving. They were a blur. It is that terrific WHAM when I bring the ball down that makes the whole thing so fast. This is a very dangerous drill, actually. I don't think I have to elaborate on how much it hurts if you catch yourself in the crotch off the bounce. I knew one kid who did the bullet ricochet once and ended up in the hospital."

In one unnamed maneuver, Pete would throw the ball up in the air and catch it behind his back, often jamming his fingers when he failed. He would start with throws of five and six feet and work up to 25 and 30 feet. In later years he'd see how many times he could slap his knees before getting his hands in back to catch the ball. The object was to whip his hands behind him only after the ball had disappeared behind his head.

"If I just lay my hands back there while the ball is on the way up," he says, "I'm cheating. I have to wait until I can't see it anymore before getting ready to catch it. This may not sound hard, but when you're slapping your knees 25 times in a matter of a few seconds, then throwing your hands behind you to catch the impact of the ball, your arms feel like 25-pound lead weights."

The "punching bag" drill Pete learned from watching professional boxers. He used it for strengthening his fingertips and for hand quickness. Getting down on his knees in Globetrotter fashion, Pete would bounce the ball about 12 inches off the floor, first with one hand, then with the other. His object was to dribble as low as he could without letting the ball stop, until it was about one-eighth of an inch off the ground and going rat-tat-tat-tat like a machine gun.

He would always finish with the body drill, moving the ball as quickly as he could around his neck, then down his body. From there it was in and out, using a figure eight and sometimes dribbling in between, his willowy body shimmying quicker than ought to be possible.

When Press Maravich played basketball in his youth, there were drills of another kind. "In those days," he said, "coaches drummed a list of don'ts a mile long into our heads. Never do this, never do that. It's all we heard. Everything was basic—passing, cutting, shooting. They wanted you to do it just one way, the same way, every time. The emphasis was on control.

There were no patterns to work off, no gambles. Just very set, basic plays. No one would even think of taking a jump shot. But I guess for its time it was a very interesting ball game."

Even though it was not the jived-up game that Pete would know later, it was still a way out of the dreary steel mills for Press. He won a scholarship to Davis & Elkins College in Elkins, West Virginia, turning down similar offers from Long Island University, Duquesne, and Duke. It was said that Press chose such a small school because a friend was going there.

The choice may have cost Press any chance he had for national recognition as a collegian, for Davis & Elkins was not only small but had a poorly organized athletic department. There wasn't even a school gymnasium in which the basketball team could play. Games were scheduled on the road or at local facilities nearby.

Much of Press's record at Davis & Elkins remains in obscurity, but he did start and star for four years, playing the crisp, conservative game he had learned on the streets of Aliquippa. His basic knowledge of the game's fundamental skills couldn't be denied. Although he wasn't known in New York or San Francisco, or even Atlanta, some pro scouts were aware of his existence, and upon graduation he joined the Detroit Eagles of the National Professional League.

His pro career lasted for only 80 games. With the start of World War II, Press went into the Navy and trained as a flyer. On mustering out, he returned to the pro game, this time with the Youngstown Bears in the National Professional League. During 1946-47 season, he jumped to the Pittsburgh Ironmen of the Basketball Association of America (the forerunner of today's most established league, the National Basketball Association). The war had taken the zip out of his legs, however. In 51 games for the Ironmen, he scored only 234 points, an average of 4.6 points per game.

Years later, when Pete turned to the game, Press would tell his son about what life was like for a pro then.

"It was rough," he'd say. "Maybe the pace and the travel weren't as hectic and wearing as today, but it was rough in a way all its own. There were no jet airliners to whisk us across the country. The league towns were closer together, but we traveled in uncomfortable buses or on trains, through all kinds of bad winter weather. But it was a challenging life. The players were much closer than they are today. We stuck together, talked, played cards, really shared each other's lives. No one had outside business interests that were as important as the game itself. We just had the papers and the radio. Basketball was starting to catch on with the public then and the men who played professionally were very dedicated to their sport, to traveling around and spreading the game. You might say they were basketball pioneers.

"I remember playing in small towns like Oshkosh and Sheboygan. Sometimes the crowds were as big as three, four or five thousand, but the arenas were something else. There was one place where the hoop was hooked directly over a stage. The kids sitting on the stage had these toy popguns that shot some kind of pellets. Everytime one of us drove to the hoop, he was shot at and hit in the face with the pellets. And no one did anything about it.

"Most of the players back then had to develop their own ability, largely through trial and error. The game just wasn't sophisticated enough. And in that sense there can be no measuring stick for past and present ballplayers. Every era has its own individuals. Even the scores were vastly different, an average game going around 44-40, or 50-45. It was still a young game and in the process of growing up."

Even then Press could envision the hyped-up scoring and the incredible moves that players would eventually be capable of. And in Pete he hoped to see the proof of his vision.

That was what led Press to stick to the game when his playing days were over—that and his wife's aversion to commercial flying, his other option. He became a coaching assistant at his alma mater, Davis & Elkins, and then at West Virginia. Then came head coaching jobs at West Virginia Wesleyan, and at Davis & Elkins.

And while he was prodding his toddler son Pete to an interest in the round ball, he was scheming to get the game properly installed at Davis & Elkins. Certain things were lacking there—for example, a place to play. The school had no gymnasium. In a moment of Serbian temper, Press stormed into the office of the school's president and demanded to know why.

"It was simple," Press explains. "They had only 35 dollars in the athletic fund and there wasn't much anyone could do with that. But I figured we couldn't go on without a gym and if no one else was going to do anything about it, I would."

So Press borrowed a tractor and cleared a stand of trees. Then he called the local paper and got them to take a picture of the whole affair. "Ground Cleared For Gymnasium," was the headline in the next edition.

The publicity was a beginning. The big job was still up to Press.

"I looked for retired carpenters," he says. "I remember promising one old fellow that I'd build him a monument if he'd help get some more volunteers. Anyway, with the help of my experts, some students and anyone else who wanted to pitch in, we had our gym within a year. It wasn't much. There was a tin roof that leaked. But we fixed that by stringing burlap sacks on the ceiling. You know, that gym is still there today and has a seating capacity of 5,000. I guess they made some improvements, but it's basically the same building we put up."

Press coached at Elkins for two years before another problem arose—money. He had to coach in the high school ranks, at Baldwin High in Pennsylvania, then at Aliquippa to make what he needed. Then in 1956, just when Pete was developing a flair for the game, Press got a call from Clemson College. "I was so tickled to get that head coaching post at Clemson that I didn't even ask about my salary. It turned out to be something like $5,000 a year and I had to coach in Puerto Rico during the summer to earn some extra money."

Then, as now, he was a warm and quirky individual, and in the pressbook of a team he coached it was said: "Press Maravich is what is known as a character. He takes scouting notes in Serbian shorthand, chews towels and tobacco (not at the same time), talks a better golf game than he plays, is a lousy football prognosticator. But in spite of, or because of, all these idiosyncrasies, Press Maravich is also a sound basketball coach."

Like father, like son. Pete Maravich was just as crazy for the game. When he wasn't playing with boys his own age, he was hanging out at Clemson, watching his father put the varsity through its paces. Whenever he could, he'd take to the court and challenge everyone and anyone to games of "horse" and "around-the-world." "Playing horse with the Clemson players was a real thrill," Pete recalls. "And it was profitable. I used to win my movie money from those guys."

To Pete the movie house was just another place to practice. He'd dribble his ball to the show, find an aisle seat and continue bouncing the ball as he watched the film. "Oh yeah, I remember now," he says. "The theatre had thick carpeting in all the aisles and I bounced the ball real low, so it wouldn't bother anyone. There were mostly old men and women, and a lot of kids there. The old men and women were watching the film for the tenth time and the kids were all busy talking, so no one ever complained about me."

Winning money from varsity players was no easy feat, especially for a 5-2, 90 pound kid who had to pump from down near the floor to reach the basket. This always amused Bobby Roberts, who was an assistant to Press at Clemson. "He was so skinny and weak looking," said Roberts, "that he had to start the ball from the floor on his long shots. It looked like a major struggle on every shot. But damned if the kid didn't make 'em more often than not."

One reason why little Maravich made his shots was practice—long hours of repeated shotmaking from all angles on the court. There was another less tangible reason, though. "I always remember Pete hating to lose," says his father. "When he first started playing varsity ball as an eighth grader, he would cry at a loss. He always said he should have had the ball and he could have won the game. But his teammates were all older and wouldn't give it to him. Later, at LSU, he began pouting after a game. Sometimes he wouldn't talk to me for two or three days at a time. He was always replaying the game in his mind, trying to think of ways it could have ended differently.

"But his competitiveness showed in other ways, too. I remember him playing monopoly or checkers. If he was losing he would *accidentally* kick the board and upset the pieces. He didn't want that feeling of losing.

"I can remember another thing. I'd always ask Pete to help us get our little girl, Diana, to drink her milk. We'd pretend to have a race and Pete was supposed to let her win. He'd do it until the last second. Then he'd always gulp his down in one big swallow and beat her. He hated to lose at anything."

It was at this time that Pete played before his first crowd. There were just 88 people in the Daniels High School gym when young Maravich made his varsity debut. When the team took to the court, fans did a double take. For the starting guard, number 5, was a 5-2, 90-pound eighth grader. He looked comical, a dwarf among giants. But Pete Maravich had worked hard to make the team and he was deadly serious.

That night Pete was all set to charm the crowd off their seats with his trickery. And though to this day he cannot remember the specifics of that game, he recalls the emotions he felt. Afterward, he came home to his father in tears, telling him that the other starters, all juniors and seniors, had refused to pass him the ball.

In Pete's next game he got the ball only once, when nobody else was free. As it happened, the shot he took—a long one-hander from the hip—won the game in the closing seconds.

Despite Pete's limited physical resources, the youngster was demonstrating that he could play basketball. In fact, he played it so well that he could pass and dribble better than older, stronger teammates. His shot was that same agonizing push from the floor that he had displayed in games of horse with Bobby Roberts, but when he had time to take it, the ball went in. And it wasn't long before this unusual style of shooting began attracting comments from some of his teammates. "My shot almost always started from the hip," recalls Pete. "When I was any distance from the basket I really had to strain to get it up. Someone said it looked like I was handling a pistol, shooting from the hip. And the nickname stuck."

Pistol was a prodigy on the court, but it was a strain for a boy so young. The pressure he was under showed up in a strange thing that happened to him just before he began his high school career. Even as he remembers it now, the entire incident is unreal and unclear. "I was scared, I remember that," he says. "But to this day I really don't know why it happened or how it happened. All I know is one night I jumped out of my window with a basketball under my arm. I ran as fast as I could into the woods, which must have been a couple of miles away. And I slept there, holding the basketball in my arms. It was really weird."

"Pete had a rough time his first year," confesses Press. "He was conscious of his size and the way the other fellows were treating him. We used to have long talks at night, especially when a practice or a game was particularly trying. I've always believed that while physical condition plays a great role in basketball, a player's emotional make-up is of equal or greater importance. No matter what your physical condition, you still need a good emotional attitude—the confidence and faith in yourself and in your ability to bounce back when you've been bad or after a loss. You need all this if you want to retain your competitive edge.

"I tried to give all this to Pete early in his career. That first year at Daniels was especially tough, but he listened to enough of what I said and his own ability did the rest. He got through it without any real physical or emotional hurts. And he was growing and getting better all the time. Later, when he would come home, we'd discuss the game in detail, go over everything that happened, everything he'd done and should have done. He already idolized Oscar Robertson and Jerry West by then, and wanted to be as good. And the only way to do that was to perfect his whole game."

Pete paid his dues in those early years, and later when critics would say his old man had created him, he was justifiably hurt. He conceded the fact that his father had taught him a lot, but it raised his dander when he heard that he wouldn't have amounted to anything without him. He likened the situation to having a teacher tell a student about the English novel and then trying to get the student to go out and write one. "Sure Dad taught me everything he knew. But he didn't practice for me. How could he? And that was the hard part. The practicing. All the practicing."

Taller and more confident now, Maravich returned to Daniels as a high-school freshman, once again a starter. His scoring increased and this time his older teammates were forced to pay more attention to him.

During one midseason game he shot from the hip for 35 points, an almost unbelievable feat for someone of his size. Throughout the evening Pete displayed his skill by continually getting into the open. As a result, his teammates gave him the ball and he kept pouring in the points.

Pete was opening up as a passer, too. He was at the point where he wasn't satisfied to throw a conventional pass. He wanted to make a moment of it. One night, while racing up court, he actually threw a behind-the-back bounce pass between the legs of the man guarding him. It happened on a three-on-one fast break. The man was overplaying him to the left to force him to throw the ball to the teammate on his right. But that was too easy for Pete. As the defender retreated, Pete noticed his legs moving like the shuttles on a weaving loom, in and out, in and out. As Pete moved, he timed the pass and put it right through his opponent's legs to a teammate on the left—the result was a basket. The crowd exploded and, as Maravich recalls, the other player looked as though somebody had stepped on his head. Pistol conceded that from that moment on, no question of it, showmanship was born in him.

As a sophomore, he shot as well as he passed, averaging 21 points a game and at the same time growing like a weed. It was beginning to look as if he'd be a six-footer before long. But the basketball takes funny bounces sometimes. Just when many of the same fans who'd laughed at the tiny eighth grader were cheering for him, the word came that Pete would be moving on. His father had taken another job.

"Some people thought I was nuts," Press has explained. "Here I was, a head coach at an Atlantic

Coast Conference school, and the basketball program was just getting to the point where I always wanted it. But I was earning in the neighborhood of $5,000 and it just wasn't enough. When North Carolina State offered me $8,500 to be an assistant to Everett Case, I couldn't pass it up."

While the elder Maravich was quickly acclimating himself to new surroundings at North Carolina State, the Pistol was doing the same thing at his new school, Needham-Broughton High in Raleigh. Broughton, or the Caps, as they were called, played in the toughest league in the state, the Eastern 4A Conference, which had already produced several All-Americans, and was a spawning ground for many of the fine Atlantic Coast Conference players. The first time Pete worked out with the team, his new coach, Olin Broadway, knew he had a gem.

Pete's physical growth was almost miraculous. He had grown nearly a foot in three years, and when he came to Needham he was almost 6-2, but still skinny at 130-pounds. "Pete came here as an accomplished ballplayer," says Broadway. "He was fundamentally sound, had unbelievable basketball savvy and became an immediate leader. The only thing that worried me was his size, his weight to be exact. He had an occasional lack of stamina and I thought that might hold him back."

Broadway had a good indication of what he was getting. "Bones" McKinney, one of the most knowledgeable basketball men around and a former pro player, told the Broughton coach that Pete already had as great a shooting touch as he'd ever seen. Gone was the little-kid style that had earned him his nickname. Now he was more classic in form. He was a threat from anywhere on the floor and had the explosiveness to score points in bunches.

He joined a Broughton team that featured four senior starters, all of whom had played together the past two seasons and had finished at 8-13 the year before. "We lost a lot of close ones that year," said Coach Broadway. "I knew the team had potential, but lacked a leader. Pete gave us exactly what we needed. He took charge immediately and, because he had all the tools, was an extremely coachable player.

"I later read an awful lot of stuff criticising Pete for his play at L.S.U., stuff about a one-man team and him never passing the ball. All I can say is that at Needham, he always followed the game plan to the letter. Our offense always had us working to the man in the middle, and starting most of our plays off that. Pete did this consistently, though at times it might have been easier for him to forget that initial pass and free-lance in for a hoop. I remember one game against Wilmington. By the fourth quarter the fans were grumbling. They said that Pete hadn't shown anything and wondered where the hot-shot scorer was. What no one knew at the time was that the game plan focused on fouling out the Wilmington big man, just working on him, moving toward him and getting the ball to the man he was guarding. Pete did this so well that by the last period we got the guy out and we had the lead. Then Wilmington pressed and everyone in the gym got their money's worth. Pete put on a dribbling show that was unreal. No one could get the ball away from him. It was really a great win.

"Pete was already a powerful scorer when he came to us, but we had a well-balanced team and he fit right into the flow of the game. I guess he averaged just a shade over 20 his junior year. Still, he was our clutch man and always got us the hoop when we needed it.

"He fit in so well with his teammates. He wasn't at all shy with them and he quickly earned their complete respect. He was also an excellent defensive player. His lack of stamina was a factor here. He had to pace himself and put his priority where it was most needed. If he had to stop a high scorer, it was defense. If we needed points from him, he gave it his all on offense. You know, I don't think it would have mattered who coached him. He worked his tail off . . . on offense and defense. I remember he couldn't jump too well when he first came. But he worked on that and really improved. Plus he had tremendous basketball sense. If you didn't tell him a game plan, he'd come up with one of his own."

Because Pete was extremely thin, he took a great deal of punishment. Opposing players never failed to take an opportunity to run into him, or throw an elbow, or just lean on him. But he took whatever they dished out and never complained. He became a good actor, too, perfecting the ability to fall, tumble and slide whenever he was bumped. It got him to the foul line more often than not, and he converted his free throws regularly. Still, he got his share of bumps and bruises. One day he was telling Needham Athletic Director Clyde Walker that he had a charley horse from the last night's game. Walker just laughed, "Don't con me," he said. "There's no way you can have a charley horse on top of bones."

But the skinny kid was a confident competitor, too. "Winning meant everything to Pete," recalls Paul Phillips, then a writer with the *Raleigh Times*. "He looked like he lost his best friend when the team got beat. But during the game he never let down or lost confidence. There was a game against Wilmington in the tourney that year and Pete couldn't hit. It might have been his worst shooting night ever. By the end of regulation time he was something like 0-19 from the floor. Then the game went into overtime. He hit a last-second bucket on a jumper to send it into double OT, then canned two more tough shots to win it. That's what I call confidence. Most kids would have been so uptight after missing 19 shots that they wouldn't have even tried to layup."

It was a pattern with him in those days. "It was hard to understand," recalls Phillips, "how he could look so bad in the first half and so good in the second half. I remember Coach Broadway saying he ought to take Pete out early and start running him around the girls' gym, just to stimulate the first half. But I don't think he ever did it. I remember him fouling out of one game early in the third quarter with just seven points. But it couldn't be called a bad game. The two previous games he had scored 22 and 23 points in the second half. Once he got his rhythm going he was impossible to stop. It just took a little longer some nights. But it almost always happened."

But the end of Pete's junior year Broadway called him "a man at 16 as far as basketball is concerned. He's already playing a college game." Len Rosenbluth, a former All-American at North Carolina and coach of a rival high school, said Pete could help the guard situation at North Carolina State immediately, he was that good. Another former All-American from North Carolina State, Lou Pucillo, became so excited upon seeing Pete for the first time that he knocked over a press table full of Pepsi-Colas, publicly proclaiming the Pistol as "unbelievable!"

With Pete providing the unifying force, Needham's well-balanced, veteran team finished the season with a 19-4 mark. Though the Pistol would be the only returning starter next year, basketball people were predicting he'd be better than ever.

Ever since Pete was a youngster, he would accompany his father to summer camps, where Press taught the fine points of basketball. Along the way, young Pete met many top professional and college stars. At one camp when he was still in high school, he worked out with Philadelphia 76er star Hal Greer. Later that day he told his father, "I just played Hal Greer one-on-one and I think I can take him."

Fact or fancy, it didn't matter. Pete was learning by doing and he was doing it against the best. At another camp during his high school days he defeated Len Chappell, an ex-Wake Forest All-American and then an N.B.A. star, in a game of horse. "It was a two out of three series," Pete reported to Press, "and it was all tied up when I beat him. I don't think he liked it very much." Another time he shot hoops with Dave Bing, who was then just starting at Syracuse, and Pete told his father he thought Bing would be the next great star guard in the N.B.A.

By the time Press came to coach North Carolina State, Pete was already an accomplished ballplayer, standing over six feet and doggedly going about the business of learning his craft. So when he started hanging around the Wolfpack practice sessions and joining in drills and scrimmages with the team, he was close to being on a par with the varsity players.

"Pete would come up to our gym after his practice was over," recalls Ed Biedenbach, a starting guard on Press's Wolfpack team. "He used to challenge all of us to games of around-the-world, horse, and one-on-one. When I played him, he didn't seem that quick. But he was a little taller than I was [Biedenbach is 6-0] and he took me inside where he could use his height and longer reach. I guess we about split even in one-on-one games. But I'll say one thing. I never blocked one of his shots. Never. He would stuff me from time to time, but he just seemed to have the knack of getting that shot of his."

Biedenbach says he never envisioned Pete as a future superstar. "I can't really say why," he confessed, "maybe I just didn't watch him enough. But I didn't think he had the speed at the time and I certainly didn't think he'd grow to be 6-5. I remember him scrimmaging against the North Carolina State freshmen one year. He didn't impress me as a better ballplayer than our kids, but when he got hot, he couldn't be stopped offensively. And I never realized what a great passer the kid was. Most of our scrimmages were half-court and he never really had a chance to open up."

One North Carolina State player who foresaw greatness in Maravich was Tom Mattocks, a 6-2 guard and a good friend of Biedenbach's. "I played a lot of one-on-one with Pete," said Mattocks, "sometimes because he wouldn't take no for an answer. Sometimes he played in his socks, sometimes in shoes, but we about split the games we played. Yet I had a feeling about him, that he had what it takes. I never blocked a shot of his and I didn't see speed as a problem. He just had some more maturing to do.

"But the thing that really impressed me about him was his confidence. Here was this high school kid playing against a starting college ballplayer and he's shooting hook shots. I never had the nerve to take a hook in my life, and he's popping them from both sides . . . and hitting them. Then I watched him shooting by himself one day. He was taking all kinds of crazy shots, behind his back, over his head, hooks from all over. I guess he practiced them so much that he knew he could make them when it counted. But I'll admit that while I thought he'd be a big star, I never thought he'd be averaging over 40 points a game some day."

Pete's confidence could be galling. One day he was scrimmaging with the Wolfpack varsity and shooting the ball almost every time he got his hands on it. Finally, his backcourt partner threw up his hands in disgust and walked off the court. The man's name was Tom Mattocks.

Nonetheless the varsity players, especially Biedenbach and Mattocks, often took Pete along with them when they had free time. "Pete felt at home with us," Mattocks says, "more so than with some of the other guys, probably because Ed and I were sort of clowns. We kidded and laughed a lot and he could relax. And we did some of the crazy things he liked to do. I can remember a number of times when we were going somewhere, not even dressed for ball, when we'd see some kids shooting hoops in a playground.

We'd almost always stop the car and start shooting with him. Pete loved it when things like that happened."

Another time Biedenbach went to a State Fair in Raleigh with Pete. "They had one of those basketball booths," says Biedenbach, "with this sharp little guy with a straw hat running it. You know how those places are. The hoops are small and uneven, the balls awful. Well, not too many of us would do well enough to win these teddy bears they had. But Pete would always get mad at the guy and keep at it until he won enough bears to get the last laugh. Then we'd go sell the bears to get some money to try something else."

By hanging around with the older ballplayers, Pete often found himself in social situations he would have avoided if he were alone. "Pete wasn't a social type in high school," recalls Biedenbach. "He never followed the crowd or did the 'in' things. He went his own way for the most part. Like his father, he dressed conservatively, never wearing sharp clothes or doing anything else that might attract attention to himself.

"Pete was really shy with girls in those days. I remember one time we took him to a party with us. Well, we figured we'd fix him up with this girl. Pete wouldn't even talk to her. He just sort of stood there in that shy way of his and finally couldn't take it anymore. He just ran away."

On the court, however, Pete was a different person. He could relax and enjoy himself. "It was funny," says Biedenbach. "Someone meeting Pete, say, at a party, wouldn't really be impressed. Wouldn't be anything for that matter. But on the basketball court he always came off as a great guy. He was always having fun, talking, laughing, enjoying himself . . . and winning. But don't get me wrong, while basketball gave him confidence, he was basically the same on and off the court in that he wasn't phony. He never put on airs of any kind. Even though he was a hard loser, wouldn't talk sometimes, the one thing Pete Maravich always remained was *real*."

When Pete returned to Broughton for his senior year, he was almost 6-2, but still very thin. He wouldn't have the advantage of a veteran team, this time he'd be playing with sophomores and juniors. And for the fifth time in five years, he'd have a new coach.

"When I first came to Needham," says coach Ed McLean, "my first impression of Pete was that he was a skinny kid with a slight build. But people who knew him told me he was very tough."

Sportswriter Paul Phillips echoed those sentiments. "Pete received a lot of rough treatment from opposing teams. Many of them tried to intimidate him physically, but he could always take more than they could give. I can't remember seeing a young athlete who wanted to win more than Pete. He put up with a lot of pain. But a loss was the most painful thing of all."

McLean was to have his troubles in his first year at Needham-Broughton (a 10-12 record) because of the inexperience of Pete's teammates. "Pete, though, never ceased to amaze me," says McLean. "He spent the summer before the season playing basketball constantly. He'd work on his skills all morning at the Everett Case basketball camp, scrimmage in the afternoon, then go to the Raleigh YMCA and play all night. He did this every day, for hours on end. When the season started, he was super ready.

"I guess I remember his ball control more than anything else. He could pick up the entire court at the same time. He knew just where everyone else was and what they would do. Pete didn't have sprinter's speed out there, but he had good floor speed. In other words, he had tremendous acceleration. Those long legs allowed him to take big steps, and once he got the edge on his defender, he was home free. I remember his baseline drive being particularly effective. He liked going strong to the baseline, then coming out and banking the ball in. For this purpose he used the backboard better than anyone I've ever seen.

"He always knew what he was doing," McLean continues. "Maybe a shot looked strange or forced to the average fan, but Pete worked on that stuff. And he concentrated. He was always concentrating on that rim. I remember seeing a photo from one of our games where Pete had his feet cut out from under him and was falling, but his eyes were still rooted firmly to the rim. He was a fantastic scorer.

"But I think the biggest improvement Pete showed at Needham was in his penetration ability. He was a big guard at 6-2 and he learned to work on smaller men, to take them inside where he was at a tremendous advantage. In close there were so many shots he could use—he had a complete repertoire, including hooks—that he made it look easy. He continued to do this at L.S.U. when he was 6-5, and I notice he's still doing it in the pros."

As a junior, Pete had led the team, and while he continued to do so under McLean, there was a slight difference. "He was our leader," says McLean. "Don't get me wrong about that. But there were times when I felt he could have taken charge more. I think there was more pressure on him senior year. His father was now head coach at North Carolina State and he was getting more publicity because of his own court exploits. I think this made Pete ease off a bit. We weren't as balanced a team as we had been the year before, and Pete had to do a lot more. That, too, could have affected his leadership ability. But there's no way you can criticize the way he played ball."

Indeed there wasn't. Still an unlikely looking superstar because of his thin frame, the Pistol was a fiery performer. In 23 games that year, he scored 735 points, for an average of 32 per game. He scored over 40 points on six different occasions, his personal high being the 47 points he scored against Enloe High, a game McLean recalls well.

"We played Enloe High at Needham early in the season," McLean says. "Enloe had Randy Denton, who later went to Duke, then the Carolina Cougars. He and Pete were sort of going head to head. The game goes into the final seconds and Denton cans a free throw to win it. Pete really burned up. He just waited for the return at Enloe. Sure enough, there was a packed house. All Pete did that night was score 47 points, steal the ball five or six times, and we win by two. He was so great that night. They just couldn't stop him. I don't think anyone could have."

Pete's scoring binges brought fans to their feet wherever he played. And he gave them everything, hitting on long one-handers and jump shots, then turning around and driving through, around and over any defender who might get in his way. There was no long hair or floppy socks in those days, but the talent was there, pure and clear. And as the season progressed he began showing even more pizazz, dribbling against pressing defenses, going behind the back on a drive, and occasionally hitting his teammates with a blind pass that left everyone staring in disbelief. But because of the caliber of his teammates, he had to be continually aware of how far he could go.

"At first Pete was hesitant to try any of his fancy stuff in a game," says Press. "He thought his teammates would think he was show-boating. But I told him to utilize all of his ability. After a game, when he and I would talk, I'd try to show him where he could have used a behind-the-back or over-the-shoulder pass. I told him the fans would come out just to see him do that. So as he got better in high school, he slowly began working these things into his game. By the time I came to North Carolina State and Pete went to Broughton, I was pretty sure he was going to be great,"

So did the college scouts. They were showing up at Broughton with increasing regularity. And despite a mediocre team with a losing record, Pete never let up. "Every game was important to Pete," says Ed McLean. "He wanted to win very badly. It hurt Pete when he lost."

More than his feelings got hurt, though. He was a constant target for the cheapshot artists and football players who fill basketball rosters in high school. It rankled the beefcake boys to be constantly outplayed by the baby-faced Pete, and throughout his high school career, Pete took many bumps and bruises from them. Yet he played on, never complaining and never allowing an injury to affect his performance. He went into games with sprained ankles, pulled groin muscles and an assortment of painful bruises. On occasion he played against doctor's orders, once against the North Carolina freshmen with a touch of the flu. He still dominated the game. His most courageous high school performance came in the state playoffs his senior year.

Broughton faced a tough Wilmington team in the first round. During the regular season, Wilmington had taken two straight from the Caps, winning 64-57, and 64-59, despite a 44-point performance by Pete in one of the contests. In the first quarter of the playoff game, Pete had his team off to an early lead, but was tripped up on a drive and suffered a foot injury. He was immediately removed from the game and his injury was diagnosed as a torn transverse arch. Despite his own protests he was forced to sit on the bench. Somehow the Caps hung on and upset the taller Wilmington team, 59-56. It was a great win.

The only problem now was the next game. The Caps' opponent would be Fayetteville, featuring 6-10 Rusty Clark, who was to become an All-America at North Carolina just a few years later. Fayetteville had also beaten Broughton twice during the regular season, despite the presence of Maravich. Without him, the Caps didn't stand a chance.

"What's the status of Maravich?" everyone asked McLean.

"I don't know yet. It's up to the doctor."

When Pete was asked the same question, the reply was terse. "I'll play," he said quietly.

The story of the game is almost legendary now. In fact, it has been told so often and in so many ways, that it's been said that Pete played with:

1. A large cast on his foot and ankle.
2. A shoe five sizes larger than normal.
3. No shoe at all.

"At first Pete was advised not to play," says McLean. "He kept insisting. Finally the doctor said that there was little chance of him doing further damage, so we taped the arch quite heavily and sent him out there."

When he took to the court it didn't look as if he'd help his team at all. He couldn't move and was literally dragging the bad foot behind him. His face showing little emotion despite constant, severe pain, he began to work himself free. Fayetteville couldn't take the ball away from him even though he had no speed. He was too slick a ballhandler. And if he couldn't jump, he was getting free enough to take an altered version of his jump shot. Working off screens, he shot his crippled one-hander. And even without his acceleration, he managed to slide past Fayetteville defenders for drives. Only on the boards was he useless. Playing almost the entire game with the painful, torn arch, the Pistol used all his skills, every last trick of ballhandling and shooting. He overcame the pain.

Although Fayetteville won, Pete scored an incredible 45 points, the second highest total of his high school career. And when it was over it was not of the winning Fayetteville team the people spoke, but of the gutty Maravich.

What next? Both Press and Pete began to think of becoming a father-son entry in collegiate circles, the kid as the player, the old man as coach. "I'd always had the idea somewhere in my head," admitted Press. "But it was a tough question. In one sense, I wanted to be Pete's college coach, but then again, I didn't. As far as I'm concerned it's the toughest combination in sports, and I had a fear of it. I knew that if we did it, we'd both have to tune a lot of people out."

Clearly, it would be a tricky co-existence. Press and Pete Maravich were strong and distinct personalities. "Press was a high-strung individual when he was here," says Frank Weedon, sports information director at North Carolina State. "Very exciteable, never could sit still. I remember him always chewing tobacco. He had a spitoon right in his office and it didn't matter who was there. He'd chew. As a matter of fact, he was always making noise, no matter what he was doing. I remember him playing poker. He's got to be the worst player in the world. He can raise you, all right, but when someone else raises, it's sacrilege. He'll yell and scream and cuss. But he never cusses *at* you and I've never seen anyone get insulted when he swears. If someone else said the same thing, there might be a fight, but with Press it's just words, just vocabulary."

Weedon also remembers Press as a father and coach. "Press stayed away from Pete's high school coaches. He never butted in or offered advice, but when he got Pete alone, he was much more critical than the average father. He was always telling Pete that he wasn't such a hot-shot. Maybe Pete made four really great passes in a game, but Press would pick out the one bad one and dwell on that. He was always out to make Pete improve his game.

"I can't really say I observed a father-son relationship in those days. It was always more like player-coach. Both were dedicated to basketball and that was the prime concern. Press is never away from the game and it's always come first with him. When he's not coaching, it's clinics or lectures, or camps. He does as much of it as he can.

"To me, Press is a great coach," Weedon continues. "He's an innovator on the court, quickly adapting to another team's style of play. Against South Carolina one time, he devised an out-of-bounds defense that caused a five-second violation, then set up a play to win the game. He's always taking notes, always figuring, always drawing plays and diagrams on the court during timeouts. And he's more of a coach and less of a promoter than some others. Coach Case was a publicity man. He could make you love a loser. Not Press. He's only interested in the straight basketball aspect of things.

"We always ran a strict, patterned offense. But I remember him letting Biedenbach freelance off it. He knew Ed was that kind of ballplayer, in fact, he called him 'wild horse' and said he wasn't going to try to tame him. He believed in a player being his personality, but also part of the team."

And yet with Pete, being himself could be difficult. "Sometimes I got the impression that he [Press] couldn't handle Pete," says Biedenbach. "Pete did what he wanted, came and went as he pleased. They had a funny relationship, always yelling and arguing with each other. Yet I sort of felt it was their kind of love. I know I couldn't do it with my father. It would be serious business if I did."

"I remember that, too," says Weedon. "The two of them were always jawing with one another. Pete would listen to Press, but then come right back with an answer or opinion of his own."

Ed McLean saw the father-son relationship as based upon respect: "I think because basketball was a way of life for both of them, they had a kind of mutual respect —an unusual amount, I'd say—and I think it makes for a good relationship."

Press, too, feels that a strong link existed between all the members of the family. "Being so dedicated to something can produce some unhappy occasions," he says. "Someone invariably gets hurt along the way because there are sacrifices that must be made. If you don't have a wife who can take it, you have to give part of it up. Fortunately, Helen had a lot to do with encouraging Pete. She used to drive him to and from practice at Daniels and take care of his basketball life in other ways. We're a basketball family and everyone has had to remain strong. We've all concentrated on just one thing."

Just where Pete would play college ball was something of a problem. His classroom performance was not particularly good and his college board scores were low the several times he took them. "You know why Pete had trouble with the boards," muses Ed Biedenbach. "Because he could never concentrate. One time he took them he knew we were playing Duke and it was killing him that he couldn't be there."

There was another problem, too. Pete was 6-4 now, but still quite thin, hardly the build for big-time college ball. Press decided to send him to Edwards Military Academy in Salemburg, North Carolina, for a year of prep school.

"I spoke to Press about it at the time," recalls Ed

Biedenbach. "He sent Pete to Edwards strictly because of a maturity factor. He felt Pete was still skinny and not strong enough to take the pounding he'd get in college. And he figured another year would give him the strength he needed. Besides, the way Pete practiced, another year would make him all the better."

Biedenbach was right. At Edwards, the team played a running game suited to Pete's full-throttle skills. Early in the year he scored 30 points a game regularly. Then one night he got really hot. He jumped, twisted, drove, ran, hitting shots from all over the floor. When the game ended, Pete had scored 50 points. "I remember the headline in the paper the next day reading, '50? Maravich,'" Pete says. "People just couldn't believe that a kid in prep school could score 50 points. After that, it seemed that people were always curious about how many points I scored."

Two of Pete's most satisfying games that year were against the North Carolina State freshman team. The first, played in Salemburg, saw Edwards pull away in the second half for a 90-73 win. Pete led his club with 26 points, while a 6-8 center, Vince Schafmeister, pulled down 29 rebounds.

The second contest was held in Raleigh. This was the one Pete was really up for. Although Press coached the varsity, the local papers billed the game as a father-son confrontation. Many of the varsity players who knew Pete were there, riding him as he took his warm-ups. "Hey, skinny," one of them shouted. "You gonna show us something tonight?"

Pete showed them plenty. He hit 14 of 28 shots from the floor and added five from the foul line for a game-high 33 points. It was no contest. At halftime, Edwards led, 50-33, and won, 91-57. In the second half, Pete just had fun, tossing behind-the-back passes, and if the fun was at Papa Press's expense, it hardly mattered. It was looking more and more as though they'd be taking bows together in some collegiate fieldhouse very soon.

The best years of their lives lay ahead.

Chapter II

In the Bayou country of Louisiana the traditional sport for years was football. It was the game people paid for. Autumn Saturday afternoons were great affairs when Louisiana State University played.

Clad in purple and gold uniforms, L.S.U. teams burst onto the playing grounds to thunderous applause and remained an unrivaled box office attraction for season after season. Large and festive crowds regularly packed the stadium.

Those who couldn't get to games tuned in on their radios. From small diners on highways where Burma Shave signs winked at the motorist to classy cocktail lounges downtown, the game was the thing.

While blue-collar workers turned out in droves for those bright and noisy spectacles, they were not the only ones stirred by college football. As far back as the 1930s, when Huey P. Long sat in the governor's mansion, football had cut across class lines.

The famed "Kingfish," as the governor was called, was crazy for football. In fact, he was impassioned enough to trot onto the field with L.S.U. teams and even compose a fight song in collaboration with the school's bandmaster.

Once, at halftime of a game against arch rival Tulane, Long was jogging to the L.S.U. locker room when an aide of his reminded him he was obliged to pose for a shot by Paramount News. Snapped Huey, "To hell with 'em. I'm running my team."

During games he would assist the team's trainer and mop the grimey faces of "his boys." For injured L.S.U. players, he suggested his down-home remedies, once concocting a brew whose base was Epsom salt. The ailing player drank it and vomited soon after.

Gubernatorial concern in those years, and for many years after, rarely strayed to Dr. Naismith's fine old game, basketball. That sport was looked on by Louisiana sports fans as a dandyish pursuit not worthy of their attention. And indeed the way it was played in the Bayou country, it was hard to fault the people's choice. Basektball was a pale shadow of the electrifying jolts of football.

There were exceptions, however. The Sparky Wade-led teams of the 30's had craft and cunning, but the game then was a "waltzing Matilda" compared to what it is today. Even when Bob Pettit played at L.S.U., before becoming a great pro, it was not enough to fire up a football populace.

Through the years that "Big Blue," as Pettit was known, was at L.S.U., and even beyond, Tiger football was on center stage. It was no accident. A great one like Pettit was rare to L.S.U. basketball, but blue chippers were common enough in L.S.U. football. The team regularly turned out players who went on to star in the pros—men like Jim Taylor, Billy Cannon, Johnny Robinson, Mel Branch, Dennis Gaubatz, Bill Truax, Jerry Stovall, among others.

Even nondescript talent was raised to mythical proportions in Bayou land. One third-string unit in the late 1950s was used defensively to spell the regulars, and proceeded with such vigor that they won the name "The Chinese Bandits," plus enormous publicity.

Given the supremacy of football at L.S.U., it is remarkable that a man might consider bringing basketball to parity with it. Such a man did exist. He was Jim Corbett, L.S.U.'s athletic director, and his strong feelings about basketball were regarded as heresy in football quarters.

But Corbett didn't care. He'd seen basketball played at its best and at its worst, and preferred the best for L.S.U. And if it seemed farfetched to others, it did not to hoop enthusiast Corbett.

He was so taken by his vision that he whimsically said after a season in which he'd suffered a heart attack, a gunshot wound and the Tigers' 6-20 record: "I don't want to be hanged, or shot, or die a natural death. I want to be trampled to death by the crowd trying to get in to see an L.S.U. basketball game." It seemed a hallucinatory scheme, but Corbett was quite lucid about what he intended to do. He had in mind a coach and a player that he swore would make the rafters shake.

"I know the coach I want," he said. "Press Maravich. And he brings his kid with him. And this kid could become one of the greatest basketball players in the country."

But at the time the visionary Corbett was plotting to bring the Maraviches to L.S.U., Press was entertaining offers from the pro Baltimore Bullets, whose general manager, Buddy Jannette, he'd played with years earlier. The senior Maravich was also being wooed by North Carolina State, where he was an assistant coach to the ailing Everett Case and where he was forced to assume the top spot when Case's health prevented him from continuing any longer.

But it was not a time for snap decisions, not after the short wages Press had taken in past years. Money, to be sure, was a consideration. "It seemed," said Press, "we were always in debt in those days, sometimes starving. At that time I asked the North Carolina State people to pay the bills I had—you know, rent, food, clothing, electricity, that stuff, besides a salary. They turned me down."

But Press did not live by bread alone. There was Pete to consider, too. "I told Dad that his life was with kids." Pete says. "He'd been saying that himself for years. Plus I wanted to play for him and I always thought he wanted to coach me. It might be tough on us in a lot of ways, but the opportunity to revive basketball at L.S.U. looked like the right thing."

So the Maraviches went to L.S.U., though the man who first thought to bring them there was not around to see it. Jim Corbett had succumbed to heart failure, but the attitude toward basketball that had motivated him still lingered on, even if one of the L.S.U. assistants, Jay McCreary, took pains to conceal it.

"Jay was taking me all over, showing me this and

that," recalls Press. "But when we went by the Coliseum he stepped down on the accelerator and shut up. It wasn't until later that I found out that we'd have to practice in a high school gym with a short floor because a walking-horse show had rights to the Coliseum until two weeks before the first game. To make matters worse, we'd also be forced to close on the road each year because of a rodeo."

It was too late by the time Press found out. He had signed a five-year contract to coach at L.S.U. for $15,-000 per year. Son Peter would enroll as a freshman.

In Baton Rouge, no church bells pealed at the news; no special editions went to press. The city was unmoved by their coming. But before his career was finished, Pistol would put the joy and magic of the sneakered game into the locals, and maybe even convert a football zealot or two.

Even with the Maraviches at L.S.U., few Southeastern Conference basketball observers expected a new order to be born there. Fans continued to refer to the school as "LSWho?" And in that tradition, Press's first club won three games and lost 23.

Losing was not easy for a man like Press. Highly intense about the game, his face reflected tension. That first year, the wrinkles grew deeper, his crew-cut hair turned gray. He chewed tobacco incessantly during practice, depositing the by-product into a paper cup. On game nights he was back to his bland diet of skimmed milk and cereal. And during that long season he took to twisting and knawing on a rolled up towel, gulping tranquilizers at halftime or maybe a few shots of antacid to ease a recurring ulcer.

Although he sometimes tried, he could never get away from the game. Advised to go to the beach and just relax, he was unable to. "Here's the pretty blue water rolling in and the palm trees swaying in the breeze," he recalls. "And there I was, looking down at my feet and discovering that I'd been diagramming basketball plays in the sand."

They were long days for a man nutty enough about the game to have a provision in his will that a basketball be placed in his coffin at his death. His only consolation was L.S.U.'s freshman squad with a 17-1 record. Pistol and the frosh had become the new attraction at L.S.U. Before long, sellout crowds were jamming the Coliseum to see the razzle dazzle of the thin freshman star. And Pete did it night after night, scoring 40 points or more on shots that defied the body's physics. When the varsity would take to the court hours later, the crowd would be gone.

In the 17 games he played (he missed one), Pete averaged 43.6 points a game, never scoring less than 30. He scored 50 or more points six times and had a high game of 66 against the independent Baton Rouge Hawks. In that contest, the whippet-like Maravich connected on 26 of 51 from the field and 14 of 16 from the free-throw line in a dazzling individual performance. But it wasn't until the final game of the season that another side of the Pistol was revealed.

The Bengal frosh were in a tight game against the Tennessee freshmen. Maravich was not having a good night. Going into the final seconds of play, the Volunteer defense had held Pete to just 12 of 36 shots from the floor and six of seven from the foul line for just 30 points. With Tennessee up by two and only eight seconds remaining, Maravich was fouled. A one-and-one situation. He stepped to the line and calmly sank the first one. But the second rolled in and out. The Volunteers were 75-74 winners, handing Coach Greg Bernbrock's club it's only loss of the year.

"After the game," Press Maravich has recalled, "I became worried. I couldn't find Pete. Then someone told me that he had left the gym alone and had walked two miles back to the hotel." The coach smiled. "Guess I should have known. When I was playing for Aliquippa High and we got our butts kicked by Rochester, I walked about 12 miles back to town. I guess neither one of us likes to lose."

"We were worried, too," added teammate Rich Hickman. "Pete had never disappeared like that before. Later, we learned that it was just part of his personality. When we lost, you just left him alone. He'd just go to his room, lock the door, and get into bed. And that was it."

Pistol was no recluse on the court, though. He couldn't be. "We knew our big men were limited," Hickman says. "So we had to go with our outside shooting. Most of our plays were geared to Pete. We set up a lot of double and triple picks for him to work off. Another one of the plays had four men on the baseline and Pete outside, going one-on-one. If he got by his man and someone else came out to pick him up, he tried to hit me or Jeff Tribbett in the corners. If he wasn't picked up, we had two points."

Maravich played hard on and off the court that year. One time Pete and the boys went out for a night on the town. Returning to the dorm at 3 A.M., Maravich reckoned he wasn't ready for bed. The others thought he was. When he remained adamant they did what they had to. "One of us hit him high, the other low," says Hickman, smiling. "Then we carried him upstairs. Pete had a slight cut on his lip from the fracas and when Coach Maravich asked him about it the next day, he said it was from an elbow in practice."

When he got his hands on a ball, Pete seemed just as elusive to his teammates as he had at three A.M. "It was quite an experience," recalls Jeff Tribbett. "As the season went on, we slowly learned what he was going to do. It got so you could anticipate his moves by watching for a head fake here, a dip of the shoulder there. Just by watching for these movements, you knew whether to expect a behind-the-back or over-the-shoulder pass. Of course, every now and then he'd do something different and still surprise you."

Hickman says, "There was no way you could relax on the court when Pete had the ball. You had to expect anything at any time. He was constantly working to improve his weaknesses and trying to learn different things. He was never satisfied."

Nor was Press. He was fast becoming a wreck from the folly of his varsity team. It couldn't go on like that or he'd become a zombie from all the tranquilizers he'd need.

The best antidote for his blahs was sweet shooting talent, the kind Peter had exhibited as a freshman. If the boy could do the incredible acrobatics he had in his first season at L.S.U., it could change things around. But there was no guarantee he could. The competition would be taller and swifter, the defenses like obstacle courses. Even for such a slick operator as Pistol, moving the team would be tough.

Pete looked ready as the 1967-68 season rolled around. No longer was he as skinny as a daisy stem. He'd thickened out in the shoulders and legs, and was lean and hard—six feet five inches, 180-pounds.

And he wasn't awed by the big time. The same fierce wrinkles appeared on his face as he whirled into a crowd of big men on a driving move, the lines changing to reffect the pleasures and perils of his bold game. Big-eyed and boyish off the court, he had an assassin's instincts when going to the basket.

But Pete always performed with a flair, swinging the ball behind his back to elude the defender overplaying him, pushing it out in front of him and just beyond the reach of a foe trying to double up. Then down the lane he'd go, springing into the air as the big men peeled off to block his way. The ball would be nestled at the hip, the body poised for only a moment. Then he'd do things even he couldn't predict, twisting into the air and, improvising as he went, playing the angles of the flying bodies intuitively, so that for an instant he'd see a way to get the ball up. And if it required shifting the ball from one hand to the other while up there, he'd do it.

It wasn't always that hard. Sometimes he could make it look easy. A dip like a tango dancer, and he'd be by the startled foe. And before the man could think, he'd take a long stride away from him. His sneakers would hit simultaneously and up he'd go, releasing a soft floating shot that more often than not would go through the basket.

Pete was not gunshy in the big time. He loved it. It was what he'd aimed for all his life. The roar of the crowd was all he needed to set him off. He had the artist's temperament before those hooting and hollering mobs, pushing always to show them a new twist, something better, different than what he'd done before. Showtime. He couldn't get enough of it.

And the feeling was mutual. Pete lit up Bayou country winters like never before. Even the governor, John McKeithen, came around. He was no crazy Kingfish, but he liked what he saw nonetheless. Ex-governor Jimmie Davis was there, too. So was jazz trumpeter Al Hirt and actor James Drury. And before Pistol's career was finished, even football coach Hank Stram of the Kansas City Chiefs would have a look. Rarely did Pete disappoint them. He kept coming up with plays that even the pros did not have in their repertoire.

It reached the point where even his teammates couldn't believe it. "It's a funny thing," says Jeff Tribbett, "but even when Pete was averaging 43 as a freshman, I didn't realize he was going to be that good. I just didn't think anyone could score like that in the big time."

Pistol scored: 48 against Tampa in the opener, 42 against Texas, 51 against Loyola, all the years of work and precision drills now paying off. He did more than shoot, of course. He passed, and some of those passes had the fans pop-eyed. No one knew where they would come from—and that went for Pete's teammates too. He was an electric circus out there, and the game he played had a crazy hopped-up rhythm nobody else had ever had. Whether the pass was behind the back, over the shoulder, bounced between a defender's legs, or simply thrown through a maze of arms, it was worth seeing. Nothing like this had ever happened at L.S.U., or anywhere else, for that matter.

He even looked different. His hair was shaggier than

As soon as his L.S.U. career began, Southeastern Conference foes found Pistol unstoppable. He went around, through, and over Tulane defenders en route to a 52-point performance early in his sophomore season.

UPI

Pete has played the game with the same intensity ever since he was a kid. "I remember seeing a photo of one of our games," recalls his high school coach, Ed McLean. "Pete had his feet cut out from under him and was falling, but his eyes were still rooted firmly to the rim."

UPI

that of the standard variety college star, his face more expressive than the cool automatons coaches liked to turn out. He was, as a pro football man had said of Joe Namath, show business.

Namath—a man after Maravich's heart. Pete liked the gusto and style Joe Willie brought to the football scene. Pete felt that stars didn't have to come off assembly lines. "Namath," he said, "this is a guy that goes his own way. Maybe he is a little different. But didn't the Beatles look different to us when they first showed up. Just because he showed up with the hair and the Fu Manchu mustache is no reason to knock him. We're all different, aren't we?"

Pistol surely was. From head to toe, he did it his way. If his hair was floppy, so were his socks. He discarded the team's white and black trimmed ones and donned an old pair of faded grays that he was fond of. Those socks were so worn that they drooped to his ankles as soon as he swirled into motion. He'd taken them from the North Carolina State athletic department when Press was coaching there. After each game, he would wash and dry them in his room. Later, when asked if they were some sort of trademark, he'd wink and just say they were comfortable, that was all.

Even the basic jump shot was different when Pete did it. Often he looked off balance or even ungainly in the air. His legs drifted in opposite directions, or hung limply. They didn't stay tucked neatly together and there was no kick of the heels upon release.

"I've always shot that way," he explained. "I know the ball doesn't spin right [it spins sideways because he shoots off the side of his left hand,] but the most important thing for me is to be a two-eyed shooter.

You've got to have two eyes on the basket for depth perception. My release isn't as high as Oscar's [Robertson] or Jerry's [West], so I put my left hand to the side to get it out of the way."

Combine the jump shot with looping one-handers and big, sweeping hook shots from either side, and that's the rest of Maravich's bag. The standard part at least. Try to catalog every shot he took and it'd be a lifetime job.

Uncanny he was, but deadly accurate too. The former coach of Davidson College, Lefty Driesell (now at Maryland), once recalled a practice session that year when Pete was shooting one-hand push shots. "He was out about two feet past the top of the circle," Driesell said. "Maybe 21 feet from the hoop. Then he calmly proceeded to drop in 40 straight shots. I've never seen anything like it, before or since."

That kind of demonstration was simply a by-product of the long hours spent scrimmaging under game conditions. Former North Carolina star Ed Biedenbach recalls: "Pete just didn't practice his shots by himself in the gym. Like most great ballplayers, he was a game shooter, actually practicing his shot under the pressure of game conditions, either in one-on-one or in scrimmage. No one blocked his shots."

The early success of both Pete and the Tigers was not only reflected in the increasing fan interest and media coverage, but in Papa Press, too. Delighted to be a winner again, Press was a changed man. Like Driesell, he sometimes found the kid unbelievable. "I don't know how the hell he does it," said Press. "He just goes out there, floats around, and in the process scores like crazy. He's my son and one helluva basketball player. Forty points a game, it's ridiculous."

By midseason, L.S.U. had won 10 of 13 games and Pete was scoring 44 points per game, the best in the nation, just ahead of Niagara sophomore Calvin Murphy. Pete had already been over the 50-point mark on four occasions, with a high game of 58 against Mississippi State.

Pete kept scoring, but suddenly the Bengals dropped three games, 121-95 to Kentucky, 99-91 to Vanderbilt, and 109-96 to Kentucky again. No college team wins many ball games with the opposition averaging almost 110 points against them. L.S.U. had to tighten up the defense . . . and fast!

The next opponent was Tennessee. Once again L.S.U. lost, this time 87-67. In the process, the tight Volunteer defense, especially 6-2 junior guard Bill Hann, held Pete to just 21 points. It was the lowest output that year (he hit only nine of 34 shots) and established a pattern that was to continue for three years. Pete never scored big against Coach Ray Mears' Tennessee club in his years at L.S.U.

Pistol came back to score 49 points in the Tigers' next outing. Still, L.S.U. lost to Auburn, 74-69. Five straight losses. The team's record had fallen to 10-8 and hopes of a Southeastern Conference title were gone. So were chances of a post-season tournament bid. For many fans, all that remained was Pete Maravich's scoring.

And that was getting harder every day. Earlier in the year Press had noted, "Hell, they're starting to bump him, push him and gouge him. He takes a licking after almost every shot. He's down to about 170 pounds and he's still my leading rebounder. To tell the truth, I wish he'd stay the hell out from under the boards. Mixing it up with some of those big bastards is gonna get him killed!" Press minced no words now. Other teams, he said, were attacking his kid like wolves. "They punch him, belly him, hold him and even knee him."

Not surprisingly, there were reports of dissension circulating that were, to an extent, accurate. "Sure, when we were losing there was griping," says Rich Hickman. "Nothing really specific, just some general bitching about the whole situation. We all accepted the situation for what it was. But it's only natural that everyone wanted to shoot a little more."

Jealousy? "No! Not on our team," the Pistol said at the time. "Nobody minds if I take 37 shots or 50 shots. I could probably shoot from out of bounds and it wouldn't matter to those guys. We just want one thing: to win."

Some thought differently though. A sports observer wrote: "Maravich makes the mistakes of the young—forcing shots, committing useless fouls and hot-dogging it all over the place."

That appraisal overlooked one thing: Maravich had to shoot for L.S.U. to win and when he did, he drew crowds that might make him mistake-prone. The pressure was always on him.

And on Press, too. Often his son was to blame. In practice sessions, Pete openly contradicted him on strategy, saying he had a better way of doing things. Sometimes, he was joking, other times not. It was a ticklish situation, and when the team began to lose Papa Press no longer indulged Pete. One night Coach Maravich told player Maravich exactly how he felt.

"Dammit," Press shouted. "I'm the coach here. I'm the one who says who shoots, who passes and who rebounds. I don't need you to decide it for me."

But those instances were rare. When the going got rough, Pete knew who was boss. In the last four seconds of a game against Georgia, L.S.U. leading by one, Pete was fouled. Press called a time-out before he could step to the line. In the huddle, he told his son, "We really need these points, Pete. Just relax and do what you have to do."

"Don't worry, Coach," answered Pistol, and he calmly went out and sank two.

"You know something," Press said later. "That's the first time I ever remember him calling me 'Coach.' "

Press won over his other players, too. "Coach Maravich was a tremendous scout," Jeff Tribbett says. "He knew just what the other team would do and could find the best way for us to exploit it. I remember when we were getting ready to play Auburn. They ran a continuous shuffle, setting picks and reversing, cutting through until someone got free underneath. First Coach Maravich made us learn the shuffle, actually run through it until we had it down pat. Then he set up a combination man-to-man and zone, which would have you sometimes guarding a man and sometimes an area. It worked. We nipped them by four the first time, 76-72. To this day, Coach McCreary [Assistant Coach Jay McCreary] says it's the best defense against a shufflle he's ever seen."

Press's savvy couldn't keep LSU from sliding, however. It took Pete's hot shooting to do that. He scored 47 points in a 93-92 overtime win against Florida, and kept "burning," as ballplayers like to say, for the rest of the season.

At Alabama, Pete got hot early and went on a scoring binge that put him over the 50 mark late in the game. In the final minutes, he was still firing away, and hitting. With the seconds ticking off and the Tigers winning by eight, Ralph Jukkola stole the ball under the L.S.U. basket. He flipped it to Maravich near midcourt and hollered, "Shoot, shoot."

"All I remember," says Pete, "is stumbling forward and throwing up a long two-hander. It went in." It turned out to be Pete's 59th point, a total that broke the old Southeastern Conference single-game scoring mark held by Bob Pettit, and drew a volley of cheers from Alabama partisans.

It was a curious sound in a basketball region noted for its decided hostility toward visiting teams, a chilliness that has led free lance writer Gary Cartwright to remark:

"The visiting team has about as much chance as a convicted rapist. From the moment he gets to town he can hear the dogs and smell the river bottom; even the referees make their dramatic signals to the scoring table as though they were playing Hamlet. It is a heavy night indeed for a visiting basketball team, a night of minimum good."

The steamy road scene never bothered Pete. He had a way of turning crowds on that transcended local attachments. More than one night he had the mobs on the road going his way. He did it by the spinning and whirling madness he referred to as "showtime."

Showtime: a celebration of his dazzle and the sheer joy of improvising the unconventional moves that the hardy pioneers of the game had never dreamed of. It took considerable nerve to throw fancy passes or use a slick dribble. For if Pete failed he'd look silly before the crowds. He didn't care. When Pistol was on the court, his blood ran wild.

"It's my style," he said. "I do it for the benefit of the team, for the fans and for myself. I don't throw a behind-the-back pass just to hot dog it. I throw it to meet a situation. I throw it to excite the crowd. I bet at least 90 per cent of the people want to see my show. You can't tell me just 10 per cent want it. Like I say, if I have a choice whether to do the show or throw the straight pass, and we're going to get the basket either way, I'm going to do the show."

Showtime. It became part of the Maravich game from his sophomore year on and made the L.S.U. road company a giddy troupe. "I loved the away crowds," Rich Hickman later said. "I'd almost prefer to play on the road than at home. There were only a few instances where you could actually call them 'vicious.' Most times they wanted to see Pete shown up and they'd cheer every mistake he made. But when Pete would get hot and start to put on that show of his, they would invariably jump on the bandwagon and be cheering us as much as for their own team. It was a great feeling."

Alas, Pete's magical game did not enchant all the people in the land. A few preferred the older virtues of grin-'n-bear-it basketball. Such a man was Penn State's John Bach, who presided over the tryouts for the United States' Olympic basketball team. Against the advice of Press, Pete tried out for the squad that was to represent the United States at Mexico City in the 1968 games. The old man must have known something.

Though Pistol was an odds-on favorite to make the team, he misfired. It became clear that he couldn't get on with Bach or play the old-school game the Olympians' head coach, Hank Iba, preferred. Talented freewheelers like Pistol, Calvin Murphy and Rick Mount were passed over for grey-flannel players who suited the tastes of Bach and Iba. L.S.U. Sports Information Director Bud Johnson had his own theory on what happened. "As far as I'm concerned," he said, "it was one of the first times that an athlete, by his dress and attitude, actually flaunted the establishment. In that way, Pete was ahead of his time. John Bach was a meticulous, well-dressed man who couldn't handle him. Pete was put on the second team immediately. He became temperamental, was late for practice sessions. Press warned him it was all politics, but he didn't listen. He was cut."

It was a bitter moment in an otherwise fine season for Maravich. He had remade the sports scene at L.S.U. and awakened Bayou passion for the round-ball game. In his first varsity season, he'd led the Tigers to a 14-12 record, considerable improvement on its 3-23 mark the year before. He'd done it by shooting the ball better than any sophomore player before him. Records tumbled in this 1967-68 season.

In averaging 43.8 p.p.g. he broke a seasonal scoring record for sophomores held for 14 years by Frank Selvy. His 1,138 points were the most amassed in a season by a sophomore. He smashed eight L.S.U. varsity records, 16 Southeastern Conference marks. He made All-American teams compiled by wire services, magazines and basketball fraternal orders. And if in Mexico City, ballplayers were dribbling to a different drummer, Pistol's was, clearly, the game of the future.

Two short years before, a friend of Rich Hickman's had come out to a freshman practice and tried to guess which player was the much-heralded Maravich. "It was really weird," recalls Hickman. "He guessed every single player on the squad before he got the real Pete. I guess Pete just didn't look like a star. He was so skinny that his uniform hung on him, and we'd all had our heads shaved for ROTC. Pete sure has a funny shaped head."

He was unknown no longer. A Pete Maravich fan club appeared in San Antonio, Texas, with a 16-year-old high school senior as its president. Letters began pouring in from all over the country to him. One came from an eloquent nun, praising Pete's talents with the acumen of a coach, then closed with a terse, "You got it, kid." Another letter was from a girl who said her future with her boyfriend depended on Pete confirming the fact that she was his sister. It was Press, not Pete, who answered that one, lecturing the young lady to take pride in her heritage and stop trying to hide behind someone else's name.

The advent of the Maravich era also brought changes in Baton Rouge. Sporting goods and department stores began getting requests for basketballs, rims, and backboards. The requests turned into a deluge and the stores couldn't reorder fast enough. The hoops began appearing in playgrounds, backyards, hooked to telephone poles and garages. And L.S.U. season ticket sales had to be cut off at the 4,000 mark so that the remaining empty seats could be sold at the gate. A new crown prince had come to a land where football was king.

One of the most popular items in novelty shops was a wooden figure of a basketball player with the number

23 on its jersey. Before long it was outselling those depicting the L.S.U. gridders.

The demand for the real Pete was just as lively. There was no way he could slip unnoticed into a restaurant or movie theater without being approached for an autograph or handshake. He took it in stride, never failing to sign *Pistol Pete* at a youngster's request. He was also taking on the look of a celebrity. Clothes mattered now. His wardrobe acquired mod "threads" and the mop of hair was more smartly groomed, brushed lightly to one side and falling over his forehead. His conversation was direct, his manner easygoing and unaffected.

It went over big with the ladies. The fair sex started making eyes at Pete. A couple of the comely L.S.U. coeds composed a little song they would often sing on campus.

> Pete Maravich, Pete Maravich.
> Pistol Pete. Pistol Pete.
> Everybody in the world knows Pistol Pete.
> Sure is lucky success doesn't go to some heads.
> Sure is, sure is.
> But Pistol Pete is so cute.
> Sure is, sure is.

Off the court, Pete took off-season trips to Daytona and Fort Lauderdale, where he tried his hand at surfing and skin diving. "I really wouldn't want to be Pete Maravich, basketball player, twelve months of the year," he'd say. And even though he rarely missed a day on the court during those twelve months, he managed to fit in a lot of extracurricular activity.

"We did a lot of crazy things in those days," says

Rich Hickman. "Our dorm was a wild place. There was always someone shooting off a can of shaving cream or dumping a trash can of water under someone's door. One time we put some dead shrimps in the hubcaps of a buddy's car. Boy, did that ever smell. We all played hard, but we had our share of fun, too."

For Pete, the most fun was what he did on the court. In the opening game of his junior year, before a packed house at Loyola, Pete hit 52 points on 22 of 34 shots, seven of them from beyond the 25-foot mark. But it was not by points alone that Maravich enlivened the proceedings. Swinging the ball from all angles of his wiry torso, he zipped passes by startled defenders for easy scores. One of his assists came on a behind-the-back pass that travelled 40 feet in the air. With the Loyola defense collapsing all over Pete, fellow guard Hickman ended up scoring 27 points.

The Tigers won four of their first five games, Pistol scoring at a 47.4 p.p.g. clip and creating plays that made great pros like Bob Cousy, Guy Rodgers and Oscar Robertson look old-fashioned. Against Tulane, Pistol managed one shot that still ranks as one of his greatest, even if he makes it sound simple. "What happened was I threw a behind-the-back pass on the bounce and the ball hit my left foot and bounced to my teammate on the right instead of the one on the left. The ball hit him square in the hands and he didn't know what to do, so he put it in the basket. Nobody knew what happened, not even the referee, which is fortunate, since it's illegal to kick a basketball in a game. People asked me after the game how I did that. I said, 'What?' sort of innocently. It was just a mistake, but the legends grow."

The legends certainly grew, and for good reason. The Pistol could, as games aficionados say, do it all. In fact, he had moves he hadn't used yet. One of these days he would spin the ball on his index finger, bounce it off his head and into the hoop, as he'd done hundreds of times in informal situations. Already he'd used his 90-degree-turn bounce pass, where he looks as though he'll pass the ball one way, but snaps it instead the other way with wrist motion the naked eye cannot detect.

No wonder crowds were enthralled. Even folks who were not inclined to basketball got with it after seeing the Pistol. Two such chaps, Bob Tinney and Woody Jenkins, even wrote a song to Maravich. Entitled "The Ballad of Pete Maravich," the lyrics told the tale:

> Maravich, oh Maravich,
> Loves to fake, loves to score,
> Loves to hear the people roar.
> Just a boy of 22,
> You made a name at L.S.U.;
> You've much more left to do.
> Maravich, oh Maravich,
> Try to guard you two on one,
> There's no way to stop your gun.
> The people came to see you score.
> Fake one man then fake two,
> You turn to shoot and it bumps through;
> Listen to people roar.
> Maravich, oh Maravich,
> Talk of you in years to come,
> How you could pass, how you could run,
> How you could make the Tigers hum.
> Arch it high and sink it deep,
> Make the crowd take to its feet;
> Listen to the people roar.
> Maravich, oh Maravich,
> Just a boy of 22,
> You've made a name at L.S.U.;
> You've much left to do.

Maravich, oh Maravich,
Play your game and do your thing;
Listen to the people roar;
Listen to the people roar;
Listen to the people roar.

But if he was storied in song and in newsprint, Pete was still mortal. In the second game of the season, L.S.U. traveled to Clemson to meet the school that Press had coached earlier. "I looked at Pete before the game," Press recalls, "and his hands were trembling. I'd never seen him like that before."

For one of the few times in his career, the pressure got to Pete. The scene of his childhood, the packed house, the knowledge of just how badly his father wanted to win put the jitters in him. And he played that way, missing easy shots, while Clemson held to a small lead. Then, with four minutes left and L.S.U. trailing by seven, Pete snapped to. He started driving past the befuddled Clemson men, drawing fouls as he went. He converted eight straight from the line to give his team an 86-85 victory. In all, he'd made only 10 of 32 from the floor, but he hit 18 of 22 from the free throw line. It was not a night that legends are made of. He was in no mood for celebrating, or for company.

"Back at the hotel there was a knock at the door," recalls Jeff Tribbett. "I always answered things, the phone or the door, because Pete had so many people trying to see him, wanting to talk or just plain bother him. So if there was a call and someone claimed to be a friend of his, I'd just say he's out, take the number, and tell them he'd call back. Well, in most cases, Pete hadn't heard of them and didn't return the call.

"Anyway, I opened the door and there's this guy in

Pistol Pete soars for two more points as teammates Dan Hester (35) and All Sanders (31) look to get back on defense.

UPI

the hall, asking to see Pete. By now, Pete's got his head under the covers and I know he doesn't want to talk to anyone. So I tell the guy that Pete used to live around here and that he and his father went to visit some old friends and wouldn't be back until real late. And I wasn't really too nice about it either. The guy just stares at me for a second, says 'Okay,' and leaves. When I go back into the room, Pete looks out from under the cover and says, 'You know what, that might have been my brother.' Then we both went to sleep. The next day he found out it was."

Maravich soon returned to form, however. His wizardry brought L.S.U. to the All-College Tournament at Oklahoma City with a 4-1 record and a chance to consolidate its national reputation against powers like Duquesne, St. Bonaventure, Wyoming, Tulane, Texas A. & M., University of the Pacific and Oklahoma City. If Pete was the attraction there, he wasn't the only one. Oklahoma City had Rich Travis, a 29.9 scorer who had finished fourth in the point race behind Pistol the year before. St. Bonaventure brought in 6-11 Bob Lanier, a rugged giant with a deft shooting touch. And Wyoming had guard Harry Hall, reputed to be as quick as a water bug on defense and tough-minded to boot. In fact, Hall brazenly announced over the air waves prior to game time that he'd "jam the Pistol" and hold him to seven points. No man or beast had kept Maravich under double figures yet.

On a freezing, wintery night—a snowstorm was raging outside—Hall looked as though he'd make good on his promise. Before 5,500 fans who'd driven over treacherous highways to get there, Hall kept Pete from scoring for the first five minutes of the game. He was in the process of making a reputation by taking on the quickest gun in satin shorts. But just when the Pistol looked as though he was getting his comeuppance, Harry Hall got his. As Pete brought the ball downcourt, Hall crouched low, hands spread in the classic defensive position, his eyes rooted on Pete's jersey numeral. A quick stutter dribble, and Pete had Hall on his heels. Up he went for a jumper and scored. After that there was no stopping him. He put the moves on Hall, going behind his back; faking the drive and taking a jumper; sweeping past Hall in a quick graceful motion, and scoring again. By halftime, Harry Hall was a beaten man. Pete had canned 10 of 16 shots from the floor and added nine free throws for 29 points. Four of them came on fouls by Hall.

Midway through the second half, Hall fouled out. But his teammates rallied and came from a 14-point deficit to draw within one point, 70-69, with five minutes left in the game. Then the Pistol turned it on again. He began driving his willowy body through a maze of Wyoming defenders, bounding into the air to perform those incredible gravity-defying heroics of his; here spinning a shot off his hip before slamming violently to the floor; there pumping the ball twice while airborne before actually releasing it. It was Maravich at his very best, a circus of crazy exhilarating motion that made the locals raised on Hank Iba's stodgy game go wild. Pete scored 45 points in an 84-78 L.S.U. victory and, in the bargain, exposed Harry Hall as a false prophet.

"He jammed me, all right," Maravich said afterward, grinning. "I went for 45 and fouled him out just after the half. Now that was just stupid of him, saying something like that. If I've got to stick the ball in my pants and jump through the hoop myself to win, I'll do it."

In its next tournament game, L.S.U. faced the host team, Oklahoma City, a fast-breaking outfit that had been averaging more than 90 points per game. A record crowd of 8,055 saw Pete rally L.S.U. from a halftime deficit. He got hot and stayed hot, putting on a display of ballhandling, passing and shooting that saw him hit eight of his first nine shots and connect with several unbelievable passes off the fast break that put L.S.U. into a lead they never relinquished. The final count was 101-85, and the Pistol hit 19 of 36 from the floor and scored 40 points. In addition, he grabbed eight rebounds and fed his teammates for seven assists.

One more game for the championship. The Tigers met unbeaten Duquesne, which boasted 6-10 twins Garry and Barry Nelson and a slick guard named Moe Barr. When the clock wound down to the five minute mark, Duquesne had an 81-74 lead and the look of a winner. All L.S.U. had was Pistol Pete Maravich.

With the huge crowd solidly behind him, Pete went to work. And, as always, he did it the hard way, driving right at the Nelson brothers. The big guys couldn't stop him. Over and over again he gave them the slip and, when he couldn't, he relied on uncanny "english" to bank shots from impossible angles off the glass boards and into the basket.

Then, with a minute left, Pete pounded down the lane again. "I thought it was open," he said later. "But all of a sudden here comes one of those Nelsons. They're twins, both big and tough. Anway, I gave him a pump fake and he took it. But just when I thought I had the hoop, the other one comes flying at me all set for the stuff. I was a pigeon, a goner. Well, I didn't quite holler 'It's showtime,' but I pumped a couple more times, brought the ball tight to my chest, and flipped it up as I was falling. It hit the side of the board and banked in. I couldn't believe it. The crowd blew me out and we won the game."

Pete had made 18 of 36 shots and 17 free throws for 53 points in a 94-91 victory. His heroics won him the tournament M.V.P. Award and the praise of Bob Dellinger, the *Daily Oklahoman* columnist. "The All-College Tournament truly has never seen one like him," Dellinger wrote, "It may be a long time before it does again."

The Tigers were now 7-1, and the feeling in Bayou country was that L.S.U. might be the best around. As it turned out, that was not so. For once L.S.U. ran up against the SEC powers, it took more than the Pistol to cope.

First Alabama beat L.S.U. Then Vanderbilt won. Auburn, Kentucky and Tennessee all defeated the Tigers. The team lost five straight times, just when it appeared to be a smooth-running club. Once they started to lose, adversity bred contention. Press and Pete in particular raged at the injury they felt Southeastern Conference officials had done to them.

In the Kentucky game one referee called a technical foul on Pete after he questioned a call in the first half. A discussion ensued, becoming increasingly heated. One writer covering the game at courtside yelled, "Throw him out of the game!"

Against Vanderbilt, Pete had the ball on a fast break and was driving toward the hoop when a Vanderbilt player came flying past him, knocking the ball out of bounds. The ref's whistle remained silent, but Press didn't. He charged off the Tiger bench, hollering, "Where the hell's the foul! Where's the foul!" He got his foul, a technical, against Coach Maravich.

In the Tennessee contest, Pete was charged with his fifth foul less than a minute before the game ended, marking the first time all season he'd fouled out. When a subsequent foul was called near the L.S.U. bench, he began riding the officials again. His actions led L.S.U. fans to begin throwing paper cups onto the floor and a technical was called on the crowd.

Later in the season, against the Commodores, an official let a defender bump Pistol out of bounds. Pete lost his head. This time he actually drew his fist back while confronting the official. Fortunately, he held back the punch. Nonetheless, he was slapped with a technical foul and ejected from the game.

The running war Pistol had against Southeastern Conference officials led one of them to comment, "Pete's got to learn to settle down. He has great talent, all right, but there are times when he's a crybaby. He doesn't think it's possible for someone to block his shot or knock the ball out of bounds without a foul being called. I'd suggest he mature before trying it in the pros."

"We're all going to miss a call now and then," another ref conceded. "But everything comes out even in the long run. Outside of Baton Rouge all you hear is how you're protecting Pete."

Jeff Tribbett thought that such comments had a false ring to them. "As far as I'm concerned," he said later, "Pete kept his composure remarkably well. He was getting worked over pretty good every time we played.

After most games there were scratches up and down his arms and all over his body. He was always double and triple-teamed, and they were always testing him with jabs and elbows. I think the thing that saved him from constantly blowing off was his concentration. Pete was always so intent on the game itself and concentrated so hard on what he was doing out there, that he didn't even realize that some of those things were happening to him. That's how fierce a competitor he was."

Pistol Pete was used to the pain. He had to be. By midseason he had a bone spur on his heel and a torn cartilage in his right knee. His leg was taped so tightly that he often had to use his left leg to push off on all his moves. His right leg was even losing its muscle tone. Against Auburn, toward the season's end, his knee buckled as he brought the ball upcourt. Press, the L.S.U. trainer, a doctor and his teammates quickly gathered around.

Said Pistol, "You might as well go back to the bench. I'm not coming out of this game. Don't even talk to me about it." Press knew it was useless to argue and complied. Pete already had 28 points when the injury occurred near the end of the first half. He stayed in and hit for 26 more.

"My knee has been bothering me quite a bit," Pete conceded afterward. "They tell me I have torn cartilage, but no one knows whether an operation will be necessary. In the meantime, it's taped at the ankle and I can't really move to my left very well. So I have to go to the right most of the time and our opponents know it. That doesn't leave me with much of an alternative, so I simply try to beat them to the right. But I'd have to say that right now I'm playing at 75 percent effectiveness . . . no more, no less."

It was hard to notice any difference. A gimpy Maravich looked as unstoppable as ever. Even though his knee pained him, he scored with a vengeance. During a three game span he had nights of 66, 50 and, in the knee-buckling Auburn contest, 54 points. In that same Auburn game, Maravich cracked two long-standing records. When he hit his 1,963rd point, he topped Oscar Robertson's mark of 1,962 points for combined sophomore and junior seasons. And later in the game, 10 points later to be exact, he erased Bob Pettit's all-time Louisiana State career mark of 1,972 points. A report of the game in the Baton Rouge *Sunday Advocate* said that Maravich was "favoring his ankle."

Common pain could not stop him, however. Bum knee or not, the records fell. When LSU met Kentucky a second time that season, Pete set still another. With six and a half minutes remaining, he scored on a soft, 15-foot jumper that was his 38th point of the game and the 2,097th point of his career. That total topped the two-season N.C.A.A. scoring record set by Elvin Hayes of Houston. After spraining his right ankle in the waning minutes of the game, Pete limped off the court with 45 points. But not even a standing ovation from the huge Kentucky crowd could take the sting out of a 103-89 Wildcat win.

But it was not for records alone that Pete played. What made him run was the spontaneity of his fast and furious game. He was crazy for the moments he could create by leap 'n twist. He came to play, and played to please. He loved nothing better than dazzling a crowd.

He did it against Georgia in L.S.U.'s final game of

It was never easy against Kentucky. Adolph Rupp's Wildcats frustrated Maravich and the Tigers time and again. Here Pistol has nowhere to go and tries to spot a teammate cutting to the hoop.

UPI

the 1968-69 season. In the last seconds of a hard-fought double-overtime game, he began dribbling around the court to kill the clock and preserve the 88-80 lead L.S.U. held. Round and round he went and where he stopped Georgia could not say. Pete darted in and out of traffic, putting the ball through his legs, behind his back, doing everything with it but shooting.

That he saved for last. With just a few seconds left, Pete dribbled toward the L.S.U. bench with three Georgians in pursuit. Hearing the countdown of the Georgia crowd he waited to just before the final buzzer and let fly an arcing 30-foot hook. The ball, as Pete recalled later, "didn't touch anything, just oxygen."

But like Babe Ruth pointing his homer, or Namath guaranteeing a Super Bowl win, Pete performed that shot with a flair. As teammate Hickman remembered: "Even while the ball was in the air, Pete just turned his back and started running off the court with hands up in the victory sign. Then the ball went in ... swish ... just like that. The fans loved it. They ran out onto the court and actually carried us off. And this was in Georgia."

Later, more than a thousand Georgians waited outside the L.S.U. locker room to see Pete, or get his autograph. And the Pistol was just as excited by that shot as they were. "I'll tell you one thing," he said. "They didn't take any films of that game, but I don't mind. When I'm 70 years old and telling my grandchildren about the shot, I imagine the distance will match my age."

And so Pistol ended the season with a bang. The clamor he'd raised across the nation was unprecedented in college basketball circles. Not Cousy playing at Holy

Cross, nor Oscar Robertson at Cincinnati, nor Jerry West at West Virginia had shown so much so soon. The Pistol had, as they liked to say in Baton Rouge, more moves than a clock.

And despite the fact that the administrators of the college game had legislated against seven-foot-one-inch Lew Alcindor of U.C.L.A. by forbidding the dunk shot, that rule had no effect on Maravich's game. He did not go into the high orbits that Alcindor did, but tinkered unbelievably in the ones he inhabited.

In the 1968-69 season Pete had snatched the thunder of the big men again, and scored more than any other major college player in the land. In 26 games he totaled 1,148 points for a 44.2 average, almost 11 points per game better than the next best, Rick Mount of Purdue. And despite his notoriety for an itchy trigger finger, he'd actually shot less than he had the season before, 967 shots compared with 1,022 in 1967-68. The tremendous pressure that teams applied against him was reflected in the foul attempts he had, more than 14 a game. As a junior he'd hit 282 of 378 free throws for a .746 percentage. His sophomore year he had hit 274 for 338 and 81 per cent.

Fittingly, among the many honors he won at season's end was one as the state's outstanding collegiate athlete, an honor that more often than not in the past had gone to the reigning kings of the Bayou locker room world, the football players. And, ironically enough, that prize was called the James J. Corbett Memorial Award.

Jim Corbett. Years before he said he had a coach named Press Maravich. And that Press had a kid worth getting, too.

Push on. Push on. That's what Pete had known since his backyard basket days. So despite the long, hard season and the glories extracted from it, right back to work he went. So did Papa Press, at the camps and clinics where he taught kids his game. It was his life. And whenever they could arrange it, it was Pete's too.

In past years Pete had been just another kid in camp. Now he was the main attraction at these clinics. During the summer of 1968, he'd logged 15,000 miles in his old Volkswagen. Working with Press in the summer of 1969, he cut back his schedule, but still managed to drive some 7,000 miles. And it was on a highway that Pistol Pete almost ran out of moves.

He was driving through Georgia when he pulled out to pass several cars in front of him. As he did, he saw a truck heading straight for him in the other lane. He had committed himself and was unable to backtrack. For Pistol Pete, this was the ultimate one-on-one situation.

"This was one time when I couldn't fake," he said later. "I had to get out of bounds . . . and fast. I moved instinctively to the left, down an embankment off the road and into a grassy ditch. Fortunately, the car didn't turn over. I just opened the door and sat there. My whole body trembled for about half an hour. I couldn't move. Let me tell you, double overtime was never like that."

It was a jarring brush with death, but it didn't affect Pete on the court. More than anything, he wanted L.S.U. to be a winner. In his previous varsity campaigns, the Tigers had started well, but faded badly— 14-12 and 13-13. Pete wanted to end his college career on top. "You know," he said, "it's always been a dream of mine to play in New York. Of course, our first goal is the Southeastern Conference title. But if we don't get it and still manage to win 15 or 16 games, they'll take us up there to the N.I.T. No doubt in my mind. New York has my kind of basketball fan. They know the game. Most of them play or have played. They eat and sleep it. Look how the Knicks draw, 19,500 every night. Those are real fans."

Pistol had real fans, too. Season tickets were already gone and a brand new facility was under construction. Basketball was in Bayou country to stay. And L.S.U. fans were excited about the upcoming season. It wasn't just another season of showtime they were figuring on. Pistol would have the best supporting cast he'd ever had at L.S.U. Hickman and Tribbett were still there. And now there were big men, too—their height had been sorely missed the last two seasons.

Al "Apple" Sanders, a 6-7, 245-pound forward from Baton Rouge, had led the frosh the season before with a 28.9 p.p.g. scoring average and over 17 rebounds per game. He had season highs of 53 points and 31 rebounds against Auburn and was looked to for instant help. "On the court, Apple is all determination," said Rich Hickman. "All he thinks about is winning. He's a hard worker, a very physical player."

Right behind Sanders was Bill "Fig" Newton, who at 6-9, 225-pounds, was also expected to add strength under the boards. "I think Fig has great potential," said Tribbett. "He handles the ball well for a big man and has a fine shot. He needs some prodding every now and then, but is a conscientious ballplayer." As a freshman, Newton got 20.6 p.p.g. and 16.1 rebounds. His highs were 35 points and a frosh record of 33 rebounds.

Finally there was Dan Hester, the 6-8 transfer student who finished his first varsity year in 1968-69 with identical 9.0 scoring and rebounding averages, and was considered a more complex figure than the others.

"I think Danny was a little cocky when he came here," said Tribbett. "But he started working near the end. He's a good rebounder and has a fine outside shot."

"Danny has to calm down a bit," remarked Hickman. "He tends to be moody and when he gets mad, it's hard to reach him. But he's a fine ballplayer."

Press Maravich could hardly wait for the season to begin. After two frustrating years, L.S.U. finally had a front line to be reckoned with. Both Hickman and Tribbett were proven players. And barring injury, Press Maravich knew exactly what to expect from his other starter. What he hadn't expected was the criticism that descended on Pete even before the season started. He had heard it before, but it was now more vicious in tone.

Some of the men in the press box contended that Pete wouldn't be the star he was if Press was not the coach. The prideful Pete knew it wasn't so. "How dumb can they be," he said. "Sure Dad taught me many of the things I know. But I put them together. On the court, I'm my own man. I have to depend on the other guys and myself, not on my father. I'm just lucky he was a basketball coach. If he taught something like flying, I'd probably be one hell of a pilot. But right now I'm a basketball player and that's all that counts."

That wasn't the end of it. There were letters from fans who didn't have the advantages of a daily column or a radio show from which to hurl their insults. They wrote to national sports magazines. One person dashed this letter off to *Sports Illustrated*:

"Pete Maravich has finally settled a three year argument on whether or not he really is an All-America basketball player," the letter began.

"It was obvious to me, and probably to the vast majority of your readers, that Maravich does not really care about basketball at L.S.U., winning or any of the other mundane yardsticks by which greatness is inevitably measured, but he cares only about Pete Maravich and what a flashy show he can put on.

"Pistol Pete will inevitably lead the nation in scoring, make All-American and lead L.S.U. to a mediocre—if not poor—season playing against second-rate teams. He will probably then be a high draft pick and be paid a large bonus to lead some professional team to a number of flashy losing seasons.

"The only hope is that the managers of professional basketball and Pete Maravich realize before it's too late that what really draws crowds and determines greatness is not razzle-dazzle, taunting crowds, referees and opposing teams, but winning."

Another fan wrote in the same issue: "Your story on Pistol Pete Maravich was both interesting and fascinating. While he may be a candidate for the Harlem Globetrotters, let's wait until he plays in the pros and then we'll see if this hot dog can cut the mustard!"

Although Press disregarded most of these untutored remarks, he did take exception to the allegation that he and Pete were using L.S.U. to further their own ends. That charge was expressed most explicitly in a southern newspaper whose writer said, "Press and Pete are using L.S.U. The university will realize more notoriety than fame from this era. If L.S.U. thinks its poor basketball program had advanced since the Maravich team arrived it might be wise to take another look. This is merely a leave of absence, which expires after the 1969-70 season. That's when Pete completes his collegiate eligibility and Press completes his package deal with professional basketball. L.S.U. is the proving ground. And L.S.U. will be right back where it was when the Maravich team came on the scene—starting from scratch. Meanwhile, Press and Pete will have used the university to build a reputation that will be worth thousands of dollars in professional ball. If Pete weren't so interested in scoring enough points to boost his asking price [for a pro contract], L.S.U. could be winning some basketball games."

Press felt compelled to answer. "Those people," he said, "who say Pete shoots too much don't understand the basic difference between shooting and getting shots. Pete has tremendous quickness and the ability to change direction on a dime. By working hard for many years, he has acquired a keen sense of when to change direction, when to take his shot and when to make the play. It's because of all these talents that our offense is geared around him. It would be ridiculous for us to play a defense-oriented type of game. We wouldn't win. Pete is a great scorer and can make the play. Why should I minimize what he can do just because he's my son?

"You know, similar situations have existed in football. It's not uncommon to see an O.J. Simpson or a Steve Owens carry the ball 50 times a game. When you've got a good horse, you use him. And I guess in that sense, if you have a good one it is your job to exploit his talents. But that's definitely not the same thing as exploiting the school. L.S.U. is our university. And we want to represent it as best we can. Let's face it. Long after the Maraviches are dead and gone, L.S.U. will still be standing."

Whatever people said, there was no escaping this: Pete Maravich was now the dominant figure in college basketball. To denote that, *Sports Illustrated* made him coverboy of its basketball issue. Clearly, it was Pete that the kids playing in the schoolyards were emulating.

"We get letters from everywhere," Press said. "Some are addressed to Pete, some just to the basketball team. Look here—Duluth, Minnesota, Los Angeles, Albuquerque, Twin Falls, Waco, Grand Rapids, Boston. Just pick up a stack. The signatures are great—'Pistol Tom' or 'Pistol Billy.' Some just want advice. Others want to know Pete's secret. They're all great. I wish I could answer every one of them."

Those who knew Press scoffed at the idea that he'd use the game for selfish ends. He wasn't, they said, cut out that way. Ed Biedenbach, who had played for Press at North Carolina State, said, "Press was a great guy and a great coach. On and off the court. But he wasn't much of a PR man. He didn't want to talk to the rich alumni or brown-nose anyone. He was just interested in basketball, and at North Carolina State, that meant us."

Another result of the Maravich era was the construction of a $11,500,000 Assembly Center that would provide L.S.U. with one of the finest basketball facilities in the country. The air-conditioned center would seat more than 14,000 fans and house athletic facilities for a wrestling team; varsity, freshman and visitors dressing rooms; offices for coaches of all L.S.U. varsity sports except football; sports information offices and workroom; building administration offices; theater dressing room; and an "L" Club room with simple kitchen facilities. The building would be available for commencements, theatrical productions, concerts and major addresses. Around Baton Rouge it was already referred to as "the house that Maravich built."

Meanwhile, back in the funky old Coliseum the Maraviches set out to answer the critics the best way they knew how, by winning ball games. This they did, and Pete never looked better. He played with a fury, going to the basket more recklessly than ever. Sticks and stones and broken bones, nothing was going to stop him this time around.

Swift as he was, he was deceptive, too. He would rush at a defender with those silky strides of his, the ball way out in front of him, looking so easy to steal. Try it, and he was gone. He'd flick his wrist out and in a blink, accelerate, leaving the man in his tracks. There was a screech of rubber as the sneakers pivoted sharply, and that was it.

What made it so infuriating for the traditionalists was that Maravich affronted their regard for the game with wild and wondrous shots and passes. In an era that was seeing the Alis and Namaths put some fun back into sports, Pete was right there with them. And if the old purists yearned for the verities of the two-handed set shot and the basic chest pass, the basketball world was whirling by them. For now any schoolyard was filled with kids who could put the ball between their legs, and behind their back, and into the basket more frequently than the oldtimers ever dreamed of. The game was getting faster and faster, and running out front was Pete, his long hair flopping, his socks drooping to his ankles and the ghost of Dr. Naismith turning over in his crypt.

He was a master of what the pros call "la-la," the totally unpredictable moves that time, place and a player's cunning determine. Maravich turned out la-la as nobody in the game ever had. He was, as the coeds down Baton Rouge liked to say, beautiful. But it was the beauty of a sleek cat that they meant.

Cat-quick Pete was off and running, scoring nearly 50 points a game, bounding off the floor on mended knees, and turning arabesques that sometimes seemed to require a parachute. L.S.U. was soaring with him—victories over Oregon State, Loyola, Vanderbilt. The Bayou people were—a sign of the times—roaring louder than the team's mascot, a 350-pound tiger named Mike III.

Even in defeat, Maravich was a stunning thing to see. Against the Trojans of Southern California, he turned what looked like a calamity into a game as exciting as people had seen in the southland. Double-teamed early in the night, he was forced to give up the ball to teammates at a terrible cost to L.S.U. None of the other Tigers could hit their shots.

"Then it started happening," recalled Bud Johnson later. "Pete just started going wild. He played the most uncanny basketball I've ever seen, hitting shots, stealing the ball, throwing blind passes, mixing it up on the boards. He did everything and damned near pulled the game out for us. We still lost, but everyone in the place came away knowing they'd seen a super performance from a super player."

Pistol finished the game with 50 points in a 101-98 defeat. Against a national power it was an encouraging performance. Pete was better than ever, and the big, young forwards showed promise. In the next game L.S.U. trounced Clemson, 111-103, and then headed west on a long and momentous road trip.

It started at Oregon State before 10,388 fans who had come to see the famed Pistol backfire. The arena was so jammed that the spectators even appropriated floor space around the perimeter of the hardwood. "They were a bad bunch," says Jeff Tribbett, "all of them. I can even remember two little old ladies, sitting right up close to the court and cursing at us the whole game. I couldn't believe it."

The crowd did not unsettle the Tigers, but the refs did. "Their coach became upset with a call and started getting on the refs," says Tribbett. "I don't know what kind of a hold he had on them, but all of a sudden all the fouls were being called at one end—ours. Then a fight broke out. After that cooled down there was another bad call and Pete, who was our captain, went to talk with the ref and got slapped with two quick technicals. When Coach Maravich tried to step in, he was hit with a pair, too. Before it was over, I think there were seven technicals called. Coach even threatened to pull the team off the court at one point. I even remember one of our aides chasing a local television cameraman with a towel, trying to put the towel over the lens so they wouldn't get a picture of Pete arguing with the refs.

"But do you know the beautiful part of it? We came on to win the damned game after all that. It was one of the most satisfying wins of the season."

Indeed it was. Pete hit for 46 points and the Tigers won, 76-68. And L.S.U. went into Pauley Pavillion in Los Angeles ready to meet a team nicknamed the Bruins, officially called the University of California at Los Angeles, and known throughout the country as U.C.L.A.

Big Lew Alcindor was no longer playing for Coach John Wooden, but the Bruins were still formidable. The Tigers thought they could upset the defending National champions, but Sidney Wicks, Curtis Rowe, Steve Patterson, John Vallely and Henry Bibby scotched that from the start. From beginning to end, it was no contest. The final score was 133-84. And by the end, Maravich felt as though he'd been through a cement mixer. That was the U.C.L.A. defense, the best among major colleges in the country. It caused Pete to commit 18 of L.S.U.'s 30 turnovers. He still managed 42 shots, but hit only 14 for 38 points. Press said the team had been traveling all night from Oregon and was tired. Pete had no excuses. "U.C.L.A.," he said, "should join the N.B.A."

L.S.U. couldn't get out of Los Angeles fast enough. Ahead lay Hawaii, where the team was to compete in the Rainbow Classic, a holiday festival tournament that John Wooden mercifully had not committed his team to. No visions of sugar plums danced in the heads of L.S.U. men as they jetted out of range of the mighty Uclans.

But Hawaii was a Christmas tale more worth telling. In the opener, L.S.U. met St. John's, a ball-control team coached by the fiery Lou Carnesecca. Other teams did not often score big against the Redmen. If a game was close in the final minutes, more often than not, the Redmen would find a way to win.

It didn't seem that the game would be close from the way St. John's opened. The Redmen slowed the action, waited for the good shot, and hit it. Defensively, Carnesecca tried a new tactic. He had his team play their usual zone, treating Pete as if he were just another ball-player, hardly defending him at all. "What the hell," Carnesecca said. "Why double and triple team, get yourself in foul trouble and wear yourself out. We just figured we'd leave him alone and guard the other four guys." It worked. Pete got just 13 points and the Redmen led at the end of the first half.

"You know," Carnesecca said afterward. "He didn't do much in the first five minutes of the second half either. I really thought we had them. But I didn't know what Pete Maravich was capable of doing. They say he does something different every night he plays, but I think we saw it all in the last 15 minutes of that game."

What Carnesecca saw was a sight that had awed many coaches before him. Pete went on a scoring binge. He went every which way and the Redmen couldn't stop him. Baseline, backdoor, up, over, he was a "Plastic Man" in the air, using his limbs like a contortionist, delaying his shot until the last possible moment and then casually tossing the ball as if he was discarding an old candy wrapper. Hook shot, jump shot, every shot he took was a delight to see.

Dead-pan Pete raced his dribble upcourt, eyes narrowing to scheme his way. Over and over, he picked his lanes with the skill of a fighter pilot. Coach Carnesecca was from New York City, and he'd seen the best of the big city boys trot out the la-la, but never anything like this.

Again and again, Maravich slipped through Carnesecca's tutored defenses, controling the game the way a schoolyard ace does in much more casual circumstances. But this was big-time basketball and Carnesecca was mesmerized.

St. John's scored 39 points in the second half. But Pistol Pete Maravich did better. He got 40. He turned the game upside down and by the time it was over, he was the best thing since pineapple to hit the islands. L.S.U. was the winner, 80-70.

Afterward, Carnesecca talked as though he'd seen a miracle. "The guy's always entertaining. He's always on," he said. "He almost hypnotizes you on the court. Here I am trying to coach my club, watching the action all over the court. And what am I doing? Watching him!

"When I was a kid there was this guy in Far Rockaway who used to be the big rebounder who would get the ball. You would throw it up and yell, 'Get it, Slippery Sam.' This guy [Pete] is three Slippery Sams. They get the ball and give it to him and he gets it up.

"He did some unbelievable things. On one play he faked a dribble, double-pumped and hits this guy with a pass off his wrist. Another time I think I saw him bounce the ball between his legs, underneath, to a guy behind him for a layup. He does it all going at full speed. That's what's so amazing."

Carnesecca went on to say that Pistol passed better than Bob Cousy and Dick McGuire and shot better than Oscar Robertson or Jerry West. "It was the most electrifying 15 minutes of basketball I've ever seen," said Lou.

Pete couldn't manage an encore against underdog Yale, though. The game was a fiasco. Pete picked up four quick fouls in the first half. Defensively the Elis swarmed him, and L.S.U. had trouble getting the ball to him. There were no Slippery Sams that night. He got 34 points, but the Tigers lost, 97-94.

"Yale did a nice job on Pete," admitted Bud Johnson later. "I remember they were all over him and almost inviting Rich Hickman to take the shot. Hick was a streak shooter; he got hot for awhile, then cooled off. He blamed himself for the loss and after the game just sat in the locker room and cried."

But it was as much Pete's fault. He'd lost the fire he'd had against St. John's. And back in the South he could not regain it against a weak Alabama team. He needed more of a challenge. "On this cold January night," said freelance writer Gary Cartwright, "playing against five sophomores on the University of Alabama, Pistol Pete looks more than slightly bored. He fairly walks the ball down the court, and a pale, shaky six-foot sophomore named Bobby Lynch steals it from him. Five minutes have gone before Pete scores, but his score puts L.S.U. out in front for good, 7-5. Now he is bouncing the ball off the hip of a defender and into the hands of a flashing teammate making a fast break. Now he is slipping in between two defenders with his double pump action, falling away as his jump shot kisses the net. Now he is charging in to take a rebound and underhand it into the basket as easily as you would empty garbage. Now he is throwing the ball the length of the court, out of bounds. Now he is throwing the ball through Bobby Lynch's legs, darting behind Lynch to take it on the other side, jumping and missing."

That burst was enough for a 90-83 win and, though it wasn't a classic Pete rampage, it was fine basketball by any standards, Press's included. "You know, I was a damned good guard in my day," said the coach. "I moved well, could shoot and drive. But the way Pete is playing the game today, I couldn't carry his shoes."

Other people reacted to the Pistol with equal wonder. Big Al Hirt was one. He improvised a line as sweet as any that ever came from his trumpet. "Listen heah," Hirt said in his Cajun drawl. "Pete Maravich will be the Babe Ruth of professional basketball before he's through. He'll be to basketball what Joe Namath has been to football. When the Kansas City Chiefs were in New Orleans, I took Hank Stram [their head coach] out to see Pete. Man, he couldn't believe his eyes. All night he kept sayin' the same thing. 'What a flanker that kid would make.' It was unreal."

Pete's acrobatics were nothing when Big Al got going. "I was at one game in Baton Rouge last winter," said Atlanta Braves catcher Bob Didier. "Pete was great, all right, but I spent a good part of the night watching Hirt. His show was as good as Pete's. Every time Pete had the ball, Al jumped to his feet and started waving his hat in the air. It was the funniest thing I ever saw."

Then there was the woman who attended all the home games in Baton Rouge. She had her own nickname for the Pistol, calling him "The Fly," because "he's everywhere." Her thing was to keep track of his point totals on her forearms, making marks with a ballpoint pen—the left arm for field goals, the right for free throws. If anyone questioned her, she simply told them that she had forgotten her notebook.

Pete's foes resorted to unorthodox tactics to rattle him. The Alabama sophomores tried with their mouths. "Way to go, Pistol Pete," they'd say mockingly. "Keep lookin' good for everyone. Take it from us, Pistol Pete, you sure look cute tonight."

"None of that stuff works on me," said Pistol. "The only time it got to me was early in the season at Loyola. This guy who was guarding me kept pinching me on the butt and running off at the mouth. Finally, when I didn't rattle, he actually came up and kissed me on the neck. Now that's never happened before. My first impulse was to haul off and smack him, but I knew if I did that I'd get thrown out of the game. So I just ignored him."

"I never saw anything like it," Press later conceded. "The kid just came up and kissed Pete, right on the neck. I saw Pete start to draw back to hit him and the kid sticks out his hand. Imagine, after pulling a stunt like that, all he wants to do is shake hands."

After his 55 points against Alabama, the Pistol was just 167 points short of the greatest record of them all: Oscar Robertson's career total of 2,973 points. The media began closing in again. Newspapers, radio, television, all began the countdown. It would take another three or four games. Breaking the record was inevitable.

Pete scored 44 against Auburn, 55 against Kentucky and 29 against Tennessee. Coming into the game with Ole Miss on January 31, 1970, Pete was just 39 points from the record. There were 11,856 fans packed into the Coliseum and all of them were there for one thing;

to see the record broken. A corps of media people—writers, broadcasters and television crews—were in attendance. And more than 1,000 L.S.U. students, turned away at the gate, saw the game on closed-circuit television in the Student Union.

From the opening tapoff the crowd urged Pete on, roaring whenever he had the ball. By halftime, L.S.U. led, 53-40, and Pistol had 25 points. He needed 15 more to break the record.

With 7:53 left in the game, the Pistol hit a 15-foot jumper for his 39th point. He had tied the mark. The ancient L.S.U. Coliseum was alive now. The fans were screaming, "One . . . one . . . one." And a slight variation, "One more . . . one more . . . one more."

And Pete tried. For almost three solid minutes, he tried. Five long one-handers failed to find the mark. A sixth was stolen as he put it up. The pressure mounted. Another shot hit the rim, rolled around . . . and out! Then, with less than five minutes remaining, the Tigers got the ball. Now Pistol had it, moving down court, sliding to his right at the top of the key. With his customary quickness, he stopped and with 4:41 left, let go with a one-hand jumper from 23-feet out. The ball arced toward the hoop. This time it was good! He'd done it. That shot made him the greatest scorer in college history.

The ball hadn't even hit the floor when a horde of kids raced onto the court. Teammates Al Sanders and Bob Lang hoisted Pete onto their shoulders and paraded him around the court as the crowd continued to give him a standing ovation. Newsmen and radio people, taking a cue from the kids, began moving out onto the court, trying to get the first statement from college basketball's new all-time scoring king.

L.S.U. was leading in the ball game, 95-76, with over four minutes yet to play. "Please," Pistol pleaded, "let us finish the game." By that time, Maravich had the historic ball, the photographers had their photos, and most of the fans had shouted themselves hoarse. When the game resumed, Pete hit for 12 more points and a total of 53 in a 109-86 romp. He had connected on 21 of 46 from the floor and added 11 of 15 from the foul line. Totally ignored were Pete's 12 assists, one below the school record. He'd played a tremendous all-around game.

The bedlam in the victors' dressing room rivaled that at courtside. Questions were being thrown at Pistol, one on top of another. He described the record-breaking shot as "my favorite," then went on to say that Oscar was his boyhood hero. "This," he said, "is the greatest honor I've ever had. I think Oscar Robertson is the greatest basketball player ever. I'm fortunate to break his record."

Letters and telegrams poured in. The one Pete is proudest of simply said, "Dear Pete: You can take great pride in your recent efforts which have established you as the leading scorer in major college basketball history. I just want you to know that the Nixons are among your fans saluting this success. Congratulations!" It was signed, "With best wishes, Sincerely, Richard Nixon."

Papa Press was as happy as anyone else. "There's been a lot of pressure on everyone the last five games or so," he said. "Wherever we went someone was asking about the record. We'd read about it in the papers, hear about it on radio, see it talked about on television. The whole ball club's been tight. Now that it's over, I think you'll see a better team. Now we can concentrate on winning." Then he added with a smirk, "Hell, it's even gotten to me. On game days, I'm a whale of a coffee drinker. Do you know that on the day of this game I had 42 cups. Really! I counted them."

Press was right. The scoring record resolved, the team took seven of its next eight games and raised its season's mark to 17-6. Kentucky was heading for the SEC title, but it was rumored that the Tigers might get a bid to the National Invitational Tournament in New York City.

It meant that the pressure would be on Maravich and mates for the rest of the season. L.S.U. could not afford to lose too many games if it hoped to have the credentials for the post-season N.I.T. Pete was used to pressure. This season, though, he'd grown to mythical proportions and hardly had a moment to himself in public. It made him turn into a remote and sometimes lonely figure.

"For three years we all hung around together," Rich Hickman says. "But senior year, Pete was different. He seemed to feel that everyone was putting him above us, and he started keeping to himself. I guess you could say he became more of a loner. He often seemed down-in-the-mouth and sometimes despondent. He wasn't as lively as before. Even some girls who knew him said he wasn't acting normal. It's a funny thing. The only place these low moods weren't reflected was on the court. Even at practice, he seemed more relaxed and had fun again. He was more like his old self. It was as if basketball allowed him to forget about his troubles."

"I really don't know how he took it for so long," Jeff Tribbett says. "Enough people recognized me during my senior year so I know how he felt. There were times when my fiancée and I would rather stay home than go into a public place. Pete likes his privacy. He really stayed cool under pressure."

Bud Johnson, L.S.U.'s Sports Information Director, details these pressures. "He was living with pressure uncommon to any college athlete ever," Johnson says. "Right from his freshman to his senior year. There were skeptical sports writers constantly criticizing him. His opponents were always trying to find new ways of stopping him, and finally there were his own personal demands. Pete put a lot of pressure on himself by his own desire to excel. He wanted to please the fans every time out. After a while they came to expect it of him, and when he didn't do it, he got down on himself.

"He was always a hard loser. He found it very difficult to bounce back from a tough loss or a poor performance. He brooded. You know, most of the other kids had other interests. They could forget a bad game. But not Pete. His whole life was basketball. And it got to him.

"Whenever he discovered a weakness, he pushed to overcome it. I remember the game with Kentucky his junior year. They beat the tar out of us as usual. In the locker room, Pete was very low. I started talking to him when he suddenly said, 'Bud, those big guys [Kentucky's Dan Issel and Mike Pratt] pushed me around like a rag doll tonight. I've just got to beef up.' And he was off weight-lifting. He kept at it all summer and checked in about 10 pounds heavier and a lot stronger when the next season began.

"During the season, he was always up-tight, worried about the next game, worried about the injuries. There is no substitute to fill his shoes. You know, he's a 21-year-old with the legs of a 30-year-old man. His feet and ankles are always in terrible shape—from the years of running and jumping. It might not have been as bad if Pete was willing to settle for 25-30 points per game. But he was always reckless, always going at top speed, playing it to the hilt.

"By his senior year," continues Johnson, "he was tired of everything . . . the endless interviews, the same questions. One time a reporter was asking him some questions, when he suddenly turned to me and said, 'Why didn't you just bring the clips?' The kid was emotionally whipped. After a game, when the rest of the team had showered and dressed, Pete was still in his uniform, trying to answer the questions. That, too, made it more difficult for him to relate to his teammates that last year. He didn't want the attention any more. It was enough getting up for the games. When they were over, he just wanted to melt into the woodwork.

"You know, a lot of it was probably my fault. We didn't let Pete lead a normal life. He should have been shielded, maybe like Wooden did with Alcindor. You could talk to Lew before and after the season only. That was it. But this wasn't hoop country and with Pete, we had the opportunity to foster some interest in L.S.U. basketball. It was on our long road trips that both Dan Hester and Bill Newton became interested in playing here. And in that sense, *we* used Pete."

It was only in his apartment or in Press's office that Pete could relax. The apartment was a one-bedroom place of refuge, with modest furnishings and very little adornment. Only a few of his many court triumphs were in evidence. On the walls he had a montage of the record-breaking shot against Ole Miss, the letter of congratulation from President Nixon, and a framed reproduction of the *Sports Illustrated* cover of the year before. Other than that, it was no different from the average one-bedroom pad—except that it was quiet. And he could relax, temporarily shutting out the sound and the fury that never seemed to end.

Press's office was a room filled with the memorabilia of his life, pictures of ballplayers past and present, and framed dollar bills that represented particular bets that brought them into his custody. The elder Maravich likes to point to one bill with Pete's picture pasted over Washington's. "One day Pete bet me I couldn't do 20 pushups. I hadn't done a pushup in years, but I managed to crank them out. I was a little sore the next day, but it was worth it."

It was always like that when the irrepressible Maraviches got together, and the banter between father and son was often on the flippant side:

(Pete walks into the office, a towel bunched under his shirt.)
PRESS: What's wrong?
PETE: Oh, I hurt it and it kinda swelled up.
(Press looks concerned until Pete flashes his boyish grin.)
PRESS: When the hell are you going to get a haircut?
PETE: What for. I don't need one.
PRESS: You look like a fruit.
PETE: Aw, you're just jealous.
PRESS: You crazy Serb.
(Exit both laughing)

But despite the kibitzing, Pete could not get rid of the pressures that surrounded him. It was no laughing matter to him when he stepped on the court, not with the N.I.T. in view, and a chance to play before basketball-crazy New Yorkers. Pistol and his teammates wanted the bid and this sometimes produced wild and woolly times in the Southeastern Conference arenas. Against Alabama, late in the first half, Dan Hester got into a fight and was thrown out of the game. Pete had one technical called on him in the first half, and Press incurred one in the second half.

Even worse, the Tigers were beaten by the sophomore-studded Bamans, 106-104. But that didn't end the action. Before the teams left the floor, Pistol went after a spectator who had been heckling him. Teammates followed and exchanged blows with the Alabama fans before order could be restored. No one was hurt, but Pete had been hit in the back by the fan he was chasing.

The brawl overshadowed Pete's record-breaking performance. He had hit on 26 hoops and 17 free throws for a new Southeastern Conference scoring mark of 69 points, 47 of which had come in the second half.

Pressure. It was there all right, but he could handle it. And so could L.S.U. Maravich & Co. finished the season with a solid 20-8 record that gave Bayou people big city visions. The wait began for an N.I.T. bid.

The bid came. L.S.U. was in. It was a great moment for the players. At last L.S.U. had become a team. Hester had matured as a senior and averaged 16 points and almost 11 rebounds per game. Sanders gave L.S.U. the brawn it had lacked underneath the boards. He averaged 14.8 rebounds per game, good enough to lead the Southeastern Conference, and topping such highly touted big men as Issel of Kentucky and Lienhard of Georgia. Newton also contributed to the Tigers' newfound board strength by grabbing almost 10 a game. With veterans Hickman and Tribbett alternating at the other guard slot, the Tigers were coming to New York with a big, high-scoring exciting ball club. The stage was set.

Though the N.I.T. had lost some top-flight teams to the more prestigious N.C.A.A. tourney, it still came up with a formidable field. Al McGuire's Marquette Warriors had aimed at an at-large berth in the N.C.A.A.'s. Finishing the year with a 22-3 mark, Marquette got its bid, but the N.C.A.A. ticketed the team for the midwest regionals in Fort Worth rather than the easier mideast at Dayton. McGuire thought the tournament directors had done it with malice aforethought, so he elected to take his team to his old stomping grounds in New York. The Warriors became the tourney favorites immediately.

Other teams invited were Duquesne (17-6), St. John's (18-7), North Carolina (18-8), Army (19-5), Duke (17-8), Georgetown (18-7) and Oklahoma (18-8). Georgia Tech, Miami of Ohio, Manhattan, Cincinnati, Utah, Massachusetts and Louisville rounded out the field of 16.

But is was Pistol and L.S.U. who drew attention in the big city. From the Bronx to the Battery, it was of Maravich that the people spoke. New York had the professional Knicks, and the people who came to Madison Square Garden were not so provincial that they couldn't applaud the artistry of visiting performers. "Earl the Pearl," Jerry West, the "Big O"—the crowds at the Garden cheered their finer moves.

They were Maravich's kind of people. And by the look of the lines in the Garden lobby in the days before the N.I.T. began, he was their kind of player. The Garden was doing a brisk business. Even so, when the Tigers faced Georgetown, Pistol could see empty rows in the balcony that made him wonder. "I got scared," he said. "I thought the fans thought the game was someplace else."

It was. The balcony patrons had opted for a Sunday afternoon national TV hookup. But the place was, by any standards, jammed, some 16,000 or more fans there to see this wiry southerner that the out-of-town press had touted as the greatest thing since sliced bread. For his part, Maravich did not want to let them down. Right from the opening tap, he tried to turn it on. The very first time he got the ball he whipped it behind his back and through a jam of players. Incredibly it found its way to an L.S.U. player standing beneath the basket. He was so surprised that he let the ball slip through his hands. But a loud "oooh" rang out across the Garden. It looked as if showtime was beginning.

Only Georgetown was not about to play court jester to King Pete. Guard Mike Laska, rated by his coach as the best defensive player in the country, was given the job of sticking with the Pistol. He had help. Whenever Pete tried to maneuver into shooting position, two more Hoyas defenders accompanied him. The strategy worked. At halftime, Pete was just one for four from the field and it was anybody's ball game.

In the second half, the Pistol came on, but not the way he usually did. At one point, he hit three long jumpers in a row, but it never approached past heroics. "There were two or three men on me all the time," Pete said later, "so I figured I'd just throw the ball around and we'd win that way." Despite Pete's lack of shooting, Laska was still impressed. Said the Georgetown guard, "I was just starting to wonder how good he was. Then he hit those jumpers and I knew he could have been doing it all day."

With nine seconds remaining, Pete converted a pair of free throws to give the Tigers an 83-82 win. A look at the stats showed him with just 20 points, on six of 16 shots from the floor. And for the first time in his college career, he was outscored by a teammate. Danny Hester had 30.

"I was terrible, pitiful. I just stunk," said Pete after the game. "It was one of my worst ball games ever."

"He played like he had a tranquilizer," agreed Press. "He looked about a step slower than usual. I think he was emotionally wiped out and had a case of Garden jitters."

Pete was more himself against Oklahoma in the next round. From the start he made the ball dance to those weird and beautiful moves of his, swinging it around the circumference of his person and then leaping to the air with it to make those singular shots. This was more like it, and the Garden mob was howling. They'd seen all the great ones and were convinced that Maravich was legitimate, too.

He was no creation of a press agent's imagination, no grass-roots marvel making a reputation against inferior competition. Here he was in the Garden, doing it all, 37 points worth in a 97-94 victory. If the New Yorkers were convinced, Papa and Pete weren't. They knew he could do even better.

"We lost our poise tonight," said Press afterward. "We choked."

"To be honest, I stunk up the court again," Pete answered.

"Damn right," said his father.

"He's pretty disgusted with me," indicated Pete.

"Damn right," said Press.

One newspaperman thought Pete was so obsessed with putting on a show that he made too many errors. "So what!" said St. John's coach, Lou Carnesecca, "Michelangelo ruined a few pieces of marble, too."

Steve Ayres, the Oklahoma guard assigned to the Pistol, agreed. "Maravich is just great," he said. "He's easily the best I've ever seen. Sometimes I felt I was inside his uniform, and he still got the shot off. He has tremendous quickness and knows where everyone is all the time."

Though not too many people realized it, Pete had taken a tremendous physical beating. He was hit in the face going for a rebound, cracked his shin diving after a loose ball, and twisted an ankle trying to drive through two Sooner defenders. After the game, a queasy stomach forced him to cancel a tentative appearance on the Dick Cavett Show. To make matters worse, the Tigers' semi-final opponent would be top-rated Marquette.

Marquette was an aggressive and thoroughly schooled team. With an All-American caliber guard in Dean Meminger, a fine outside shooter in Jeff Sewell, and rebounders Ric Cobb, Joe Thomas and Gary Brell, the Warriors would be tough to beat. Both Meminger and Cobb were products of the city's playgrounds and

A tense moment for father and son at the N.I.T. in Pete's senior year. Though they often argued about how the game should be played, Pete always looked to Press for help when things got tough.

UPI

College basketball's *Player of the Year* contemplates his professional future after receiving the *Naismith Award* in *March of 1970.*

UPI

Coach McGuire was a native himself. They had plenty of fans in New York.

McGuire's kids reflected the cocksure combativeness their coach had had in the pros. Not as talented as his teammate-brother, Dick McGuire, Al nevertheless had managed to stay in the pros for several seasons, making up in fiery intensity what he lacked in godgiven abilities. The Warriors played defense the way their coach did, quick and slashing and aggressive. They were not awed by anybody. Maravich could expect them to come after him like street fighters.

Meanwhile, up in his hotel room, he was having enough troubles. "The phone kept ringing all the time," Tribbett says. "We left word at the desk not to let any phone calls through, but they kept coming. Everyone wanted Pete. Writers, fans, kooks. After the Oklahoma game, Pete and I stayed up all night and just reminisced about our four years together. One night, about 2:30 A.M., a girl knocked on the door and kept calling Pete's name, drawing it out, 'Peeeeeeeete, Peeeeeeeete.' He was all ready to go into the hall when she disappeared. It was impossible."

Not nearly as impossible as Marquette made it for him on the court. Wherever he turned that night, Warriors were sure to follow. The dimensions of the court seemed to shrink when he got the ball. It was like operating out of a phone booth. Battered and weary from previous games, he tried to make a go of it. But it wasn't his night, and less so the Tigers'.

Meminger and Sewell pinioned him in the corners of the floor, and forced him to give up the ball. When he tried to spin away from them, he was hindered by a bum ankle. At times, he actually limped as he ran.

Meantime, Marquette was controlling the boards so thoroughly that they were sometimes getting two and three shots.

"We played like a bunch of fifth-grade kids," said Press later. "My guys were up till all hours, watching TV until two or three in the morning. You have a choice of 17,000 channels up here. When they'd get up in the morning, they looked like they were on a seven-day drunk."

McGuire's defense had something to do with it, too. His club was using a combination defense—part zone and part man-to-man. Pistol never went anywhere without a Warrior on him, and often two. The bigger Marquette players operated out of a zone-type triangle, shifting with the ball rather than a specific man.

When Pete hit a jumper with 1:12 remaining in the game, the Marquette fans gave a mocking cheer. He had gone almost 19 minutes without a field goal, finishing with 20 points for the night, not nearly enough to hold back Marquette. L.S.U. lost, 101-79. To rub salt into the wound, Marquette's Meminger said afterward, "I see better players on the New York City playground all the time."

Added reserve guard Jack Burke, "I'll play pro ball for cab fare and a hamburger if they just let me play Maravich every night."

It was the hour of the crows. Indeed the Marquette team had undermined Pete's game so completely that there was cause to celebrate. But in the slights they dealt his ability they were shouting down an endless corridor. For in the flashes of brilliance Pistol managed, it was transparently clear to basketball observers that Pete Maravich was down but not nearly out. Only a fool would say so. After all, he'd scored 44.5 p.p.g. his senior year, a total of 3,667 in a three year L.S.U. career, and in that time he'd done it before 800,000 fans. If it bothered Pistol Pete that he couldn't light up the Garden the way he wanted, it did not shatter him. He'd be back.

"People have said he's too cocky sometimes," said Press. "But a superplayer has to have superconfidence. All the great ones have it.

"We have a saying. We remind ourselves of it all the time, so that things never get out of perspective—"peacock today, feathers tomorrow."

Chapter III

What price Maravich?

That was the burning question in basketball circles once school days were over in the Bayou. Clearly, the price was going to be higher than the heavens.

In smoke-filled rooms men now figured out ways to get Maravich to play for pay. It was no longer simply a matter of straight cash. These days fringe considerations were part of a deal—like payments spread out over the years to take the tax bite off. It was a players' market and the stars could make big demands.

And no question, Pete Maravich had star quality that would pay off for a team at the box office. He put fun in the game and made it matter to even the marginal fan. It was a very marketable gift.

He also could play like a demon, and pro basketball people figured he'd keep doing so. "In fact," said former Boston Celtic great "Easy" Ed Macauley, "I'm sure Pete will be a much better pro than a college ballplayer. He won't get as many points, but that doesn't matter. It's more important he land with the right team, one that has the blend of ballplayers to bring out his extraordinary qualities.

"He does things on the court that you want to see again, because you just don't believe it. I remember seeing him against Kentucky. He did something that made me shake my head. It would have done the same to Red Auerbach, Red Holzman or Richie Guerin. He was dribbling up court right-handed, went between his legs with it, then picked it up with his left hand, dribbled clear and connected on as pretty a left-handed hook as you'll ever see.

"I haven't seen a ball-handler like him since the heyday of Bob Cousy and Dick McGuire. He can do the same thing as those two guys, rip a team to shreds with his passes. His real advantage is in his shooting. Cousy and McGuire both had limitations. Not Pete. He can hit from long or short range, right or left-handed. There isn't a shot he can't make."

Papa Press made it clear what he thought the pros were getting: "He's the most exciting player there ever was. If you want a comparison, let's take a guy like Rick Barry, who was a great college player. Pete can do more things than Barry ever dreamed of doing. Barry was just a shooter in college. He couldn't carry Pete's shoes as a ball-handler. I'd really love to see Pete in there with a 6-10 or 7-foot center who could get the ball for him. Then you'd probably see the damndest ball handling that ever took place. Will he make it in the pros? He'll make it as big as anyone ever did."

Press didn't have to pitch that hard for the contract.

The N.B.A. and A.B.A. were waging a dollar war that made the players' agents practically leer.

For Pete, money spoke, but he preferred that it have a southern accent. "If I play pro ball, it'll have to be in the south. I was raised there, I love the people, the fans, the environment and the prospects of a future life there."

That gave the newer league, the A.B.A., a fighting chance at landing Maravich. It had a highly solvent franchise in the Carolina Cougars and the team owner, Jim Gardner, was known as a go-getter. A hamburger franchise magnate and a U.S. Congressman at age 32, he managed to get the rights to Maravich and then began wooing him.

Back in the N.B.A. a series of strange events were occurring that would end up giving Pete the chance to play in his beloved southlands for that league if he wished. It started innocently enough when San Francisco Warrior owner Franklin Mieuli tried to get the negotiating rights to former Atlanta Hawk center Zelmo Beaty, a move that would keep the team in pivot play should the injury-prone San Francisco center, Nate Thurmond, fail to recover from knee surgery. Beaty had jumped to the A.B.A. a season earlier, but it was rumored he was pondering a return to the N.B.A. The Hawks granted Mieuli the rights he wanted and got in return a "player to be named at a later date." An option gave them the choice of exercising the Warriors' first draft choice if they wanted.

Atlanta took the option—the third pick in the pro draft that year. But it seemed unlikely that the Hawks would get Maravich. Detroit had the first choice and selected 6-11 center Bob Lanier, hoping to solve a long-standing pivot problem. San Diego was next and was expected to choose Maravich. But apparently the Rockets thought better of it, figuring that their shot-hungry pivotman, Elvin Hayes, might not be disposed to play with the Pistol. Atlanta went for Pete quicker than you could say Rudy Tomjanovich, the man San Diego took over Maravich.

Suddenly the N.B.A. was in the thick of the negotiations. Even Press conceded that the N.B.A. had a fine chance of getting the kid. "I think," he said, "that somewhere in his heart, he still wants to play against his boyhood idols, Oscar Robertson and Jerry West."

The league's economic solvency didn't hurt either. Rumor had it that Pete wasn't entirely sold on the A.B.A. as a lasting entity. And when the N.B.A. guaranteed a pension for 30 years, there was little doubt that the league could deliver.

Down in Carolina, Jim Gardner was scrambling. He had the wires burning to Press Maravich's office and, to make his deal more attractive to him, offered food franchises. It was not the magic word to Press. He'd had a financially bad experience in fried chicken outlets in Baton Rouge not so long before. He put Gardner off awhile and listened to what the N.B.A. had to say.

That put Gardner in a fighting mood. He phoned up Hal Hayes of the *Atlanta Constitution* and said, "The Hawks will think that Quantrill's Raiders were a bunch of amateurs if they luck out and sign Maravich. If the Cougars don't get him, we're going to put all the money in a hat, call up Lou Hudson and Walt Hazzard [two Hawks stars] and tell them it's theirs for the taking. They'll listen to us."

In the meantime he did nothing to dissuade the

Maraviches from going to the N.B.A. "The more my attorneys told me about the negotiations with the Hawks, the better it looked," Press has recalled. "It was a more solid deal. Carolina was talking about food franchises, while the Hawks were concentrating on deferred income and real estate."

On the evening of March 26, in the Tara Room I of Atlanta's posh Mariott Hotel, cameras whirred and reporters scribbled when Maravich's lawyer, Les Zittrain, strode up to a microphone. "We are most happy to announce," he said, "that Pete Maravich will play professional basketball for the Atlanta Hawks..."

The details went something like this. Pete's contract was estimated at between 1.6 and 2 million dollars, most of which would be paid over a five-year period. The Pistol would receive more than $300,000 per year, of which just $40,000 would be considered salary. He also got a new Plymouth GTX, a country club membership and an Atlanta apartment. And for the record, Hawk owner Tom Cousins didn't think the price was too high. "I remember watching Sandy Koufax pitch one day," he said. "It was the same year he held out and threatened to sit out the entire season. Well, here he was, pitching in Atlanta and the stands were packed. Right then I figured the guy was paying his salary. He paid it every time he pitched."

The moment Pete signed, the pressure was on. The money made it so, plus the fame that preceded him.

To the pros, Maravich was just the new kid on the block. "They like to take advantage of skinny people around here," said teammate Joe Caldwell. "I was just 185 pounds when I came up. It didn't take me long to learn. I'm at 210 now and I need every pound of it."

"You can't call him just another rookie, let's face it," said Atlanta coach Richie Guerin. "But I've got to treat him as I would any other rookie. They all have to prove they can do it on the court. Even Alcindor. He had the pressure on him last year. And Pete's going to have plenty of it this year."

Not all the pressure would be in the wars he'd have to fight on the court. He'd have to prove himself to his own teammates too, most of whom had not gotten the kind of money Maravich had on entering the pros.

The pro game was strange that way. It required a coach to be a psychiatrist as well as a tactician. For money made men possessive about the ball and at times unconcerned for the team concept. It took delicate juggling to keep a team intact and not let the powerful egos of the players ruin it.

San Diego was a case in point. The team's star, Elvin Hayes—the "Big E" on your sporting pages—was notorious for tantrums when he felt he wasn't getting the ball. Often he berated teammates during games if he didn't get his shots. During one game, San Diego writer Bud Maloney kept a chart that showed Hayes had shot the ball 28 of 29 times he had had it. Later, when team captain Don Kojis and Hayes bickered about a diary Kojis kept that ennumerated the E's quirks, management solved its problem. They traded Kojis and kept Hayes, overlooking his temper for the grandeur of his shots.

When 6-8 Connie Hawkins came to Phoenix after a long exile in other leagues, he was expected to be the hub of the attack. But the team's leading scorer before him, 6-1 Gail Goodrich, was not inclined to shoot less often than he had before. And the team became divided over whether Goodrich was self-serving or not. Management resolved the problem after the season by trading Goodrich to the Lakers—like San Diego, preferring to keep its bigger man.

For an N.B.A. rookie, the politics that most clubs experience just made his job harder. He had to discover the way the winds blew and learn to go with them. To buck them might make waves he'd regret. If he had signed for big money, he risked becoming a source of discontent among his teammates, particularly if he did not seem to be worth every penny from the start. In the N.B.A. that was often the case with highly touted college stars coming into the league. It took time to get used to the pro game.

In the meantime the veteran players who'd battled years for their place were reminded of their struggle every time the well-heeled rookie miscued. It could become a very ugly thing. When Cazzie Russell was a rookie with the New York Knicks, it had happened to him. A teammate became so obsessed by Russell's substantial contract that a grudge developed. The teammate wouldn't pass him the ball and talked all the time behind his back. In time the man was traded.

In Maravich's case, the ballyhoo was even greater. In his three years at L.S.U., he received more attention than any player in history. He knew there would be pressure, but he was ready. "In my opinion," he said, "the professional basketball player is the greatest athlete in the world. Every rookie coming into the league has to learn through experience. I'm just a rookie, but I'm going to work hard. It's not an easy road to ride, but with hard work and determination, I should survive.

And there are always new players coming up to keep you running scared.

"As a rookie, I'd love to break into the starting lineup. But it isn't easy for a rookie to start, no matter who he is or what he did in college. I just hope that my overall ability, coupled with hard work, dedication, desire and determination, will help me crack the lineup."

It wouldn't be as simple as that. There was another matter. Pete was white. The first seven Hawk players were black. While he wouldn't be branded a "honky," he was still bound to be more alien than if he'd been a "brother." It was a far cry from the days when Press Maravich played with the Pittsburgh Ironmen. Then players were a close-knit, dedicated bunch. They were that way no longer. One reason why teams were not as close was that the bigger dollar kept players busy in their outside interests. The other reason was the predominance of blacks. There weren't any when Press Maravich was taking 30-foot set shots for the Ironmen. Now, there were more blacks than whites playing.

The easy comraderie that once existed within teams could no longer be taken for granted. Former N.B.A. star Dolph Shayes remembers, "There'd be a black on one team and a black on another. Maybe they never met before in their lives, but they'd talk for just a few minutes and it would seem they were lifelong friends."

The Knicks' Dick Barnett put it this way to writer Phil Berger: "There are so many forces. You have the environmental force, you have the forces of culture, you know, you got so many things. Like I want to see 'Sly and the Family Stone.' Like, the white players, they aren't hip to that. That's not in their world, you know ... they're apart from it. They might go see Johnny Cash. I can't dig him. There are so many things. Like, most white players don't dance, they don't know how to dance. In our world, they're considered squares and maybe they'd feel inadequate in our world if they did try to hang out with us. We had a couple of dances where a couple of [white] guys tried to dance. They just ... they were out of their class, let's put it like that. I mean, like, it's what do you have in common except playing basketball?"

What they had in common was the pursuit of the almighty dollar and when Pete got his so easily, it was bound to rankle some teammates. His money was more discussed than his ability. When *Atlanta Constitution* sportwriter George Cunningham went out on the streets to question fans about Pistol, it was the cold cash they kept referring to.

An Atlanta salesman told Cunningham: "I'm in favor of the tryout system. First, let all rookies try to make the team. If they succeed, pay all of them the same minimum wage. Then if they succeed, pay them what they are worth. You know, the loss of Vince Lombardi didn't kill the Packers. They started dying when they signed Donnie Anderson and Jim Grabowski to big bonus contracts. It wasn't long after that many of their veteran mainstays, men who were making much less, started retiring."

Another local resident said that the Braves' Henry Aaron was one of the few athletes who actually earned his $100,000 salary. Comparing the rightfielder to Maravich, he said, "This contract seems like a lot of money for an untried player. When you perfect a player to a certain point and then overpay him, the player will lay down on you because he has nothing to shoot for. It's just like a dog race. You have to keep something in front of the competitor to keep him running."

Most people seemed to be against the big money. But no doubt it appealed to the dreamer in every one of them. One shoe store operator admitted as much, saying, "A big bonus might start a young fellow on the wrong road of life. But it sure wouldn't hurt an old man like me."

In down-to-earth terms it was, as Coach Richie Guerin put it, "Complete insanity." He said, "Kids coming out of school don't deserve one-fourth, no, one-twentieth of what they're getting. But a team has an obligation to its players and fans, and must try to sign the available talent. But the value and prices on some of the players is pure insanity."

Yet one fact remained. Maravich would pack the stands of the dimly lit Alexander Memorial Coliseum, where Atlanta played its home games. And he'd be a draw on the road too. Like Ali and Namath, he had the flash that made men care. They'd come to jeer or cheer him. But they'd come. In Cunningham's survey, 36 of 50 people questioned said they planned to see Maravich play, and 26 of these admitted they'd never seen a Hawk game before. Typical was one 19-year-old who said, "I've got to see just how good this cat really is. I've never gone to a Hawk game, but you can bet I'm going now."

There was a time in the history of the Hawks when its teams drew no fans at all. The franchise had started in Milwaukee in 1951. The Milwaukee Hawks were basketball's early version of the Cleveland Cavaliers. Coaching the team in those early days was Red

Holzman, later to become the coach and general manager of the New York Knicks. Holzman tried every trick he knew to fire up his team. He even showed a picture of his youngest daughter in pre-game meetings, pleading with his team, "Just look at her, fellows. What's going to become of this sweet little thing if we don't win ball games." It didn't work. The team won 83 of 203 games and Holzman got the axe.

Perhaps the Holzman era is best typified by an incident that occurred toward the end of his regime there. As usual, the Hawks were losing and taking a terrific beating on the boards. At halftime, while trying to realign his defense, Holzman noticed Frank Selvy dozing against his locker. "Frank, wake up!" the coach barked. "Where are we losing this game?" The sleepy-eyed Selvy thought for a while, then answered, "Well, Coach, I'd say we're losing the game right here in Milwaukee."

That wasn't all. Another Hawk coach began scheduling practices at strange times, like nine o'clock in the morning. It wasn't until later that it was learned that to satisfy his wife's demands for equal time he would schedule his team's sessions only after she outlined her plans. It go so bad that the coach was late to a pre-game ceremony honoring him. It turned out he was chauffeuring his wife around town. One of the marriages had to end. It was the one to the team.

It was not easy to coach those early Hawk teams. Slater Martin tried to double as player and coach. It was so trying that he couldn't remember the plays he had devised at the pre-game meeting. Exit another coach.

When the team moved to St. Louis in 1955, it finally

started to straighten out. It was the era of the great Bob Pettit. The Hawks took five straight conference titles from 1956-60 and an N.B.A. championship in the 1957-58 season.

In May of 1968, the team moved to Atlanta. Flamboyant owner Ben Kerner had sold his interest in the team to Thomas Cousins, an Atlanta businessman and Carl Sanders, the former governor of the state. The proposed move south was greeted with skepticism. Atlanta fans hadn't expressed a strong desire for a professional basketball team and there was no real facility in which the team could play. One problem was solved when the Hawks received permission to play in Alexander Memorial Coliseum on the Georgia Tech Campus. The second was solved when the city became acquainted with the team. With transplanted New Yorker Richie Guerin as coach, and ever-improving personnel, the Hawks played to identical 48-34 records for their first two seasons in Atlanta, finishing second and then first in the N.B.A. west. But both seasons the team was beaten in the playoffs. Yet Atlanta remained a close-knit, prideful unit. The future looked bright.

The Hawk captain was Bill Bridges, a burly 6-6, 235-pound forward who managed to get rebounds even against the taller men playing beneath the boards. In 1969-70, he was fourth best in the league with 1,181 caroms. "There's no real secret to rebounding," Bridges says. "You simply have to get your position and hold it, using everything . . . your back, your shoulders, your arms, your butt, your legs. You've got to keep the other guy behind you. Get that position and hold it." In a league where rough play can be intimidating, Bridges kept the foe "honest."

"Sweet Lou"—that's what they called Lou Hudson. His gamebreaking jump shot had earned him that nickname during his career at the University of Minnesota. The Hawks first draft choice in 1966, the 6-5 Hudson played forward in 1968-69 and averaged 21.9 points in an all-star year. Switching to guard the next season, he hit for 25.3 p.p.g. and was named to the All-Pro team.

There is a statistic in the Hawk record book that best relates the value of Lou Hudson. It says that when Hudson takes 20 or more shots a game, the Hawks win 80 per cent of the time. When he shoots less, the team loses more than it wins. Sweet Lou. The shooter.

"Pogo Joe" on the Hawks was not the team mascot. He was Joe Caldwell, called Pogo because he could leap automobiles in a single bound. He did that for kicks at Arizona State where he became an All-American. Moved from guard to forward in the pros, he played with great flair, soaring through the air with the majesty of eagles. He scored when he soared, better than 20 p.p.g., and his speed made the Hawks run. When he wanted to, and he almost always did, he was a superb defender, good enough to make the N.B.A. All-Defense team.

Walt Hazzard, a 6-3 guard, was known as "The Wizzard" to his teammates. He came to the Hawks in a controversial trade that sent popular Lenny Wilkins to Seattle. Hazzard had averaged 23.9 points for the expansion Supersonics in 1967-68. But in Wilkens' place as floor leader of the Hawks the next year, he faltered. During the off-season, he spent hours with the video tape machine, seeking ways to improve his game. The next year he did, leading the club with 561 assists, scoring at a 15.3 clip, and tying a club record with 24 points in one quarter against San Diego.

"There were times when I wondered what would happen," Hazzard said. "I came here and right away people expected me to perform like Lennie. At Seattle I was primarily a shooter. Here, I was expected to run the club from A to Z. The pressure was on, man, and it took me one whole season to work it out."

The center was Walter Bellamy, "Big Bells." He had come out of the University of Indiana in 1961 as a 6-11, 245-pounder. His first year at Chicago he scored 31.6 p.p.g. and grabbed 1,500 rebounds. Those statistics remain his best in a nine-year career. Endowed with speed, jumping ability and a good shot, Bellamy had all the ingredients to be among the best. But his frequent lackluster play puzzled analysts. One time in Detroit he didn't even join the huddle during a time-out. When he finally meandered over, his replacement had already checked into the game. Another time he came off the bench and promptly scored 22 points, inciting a teammate to remark, "Gee, Walt. I thought you'd retired."

At Atlanta, Big Bells found himself on a team headed for the division championship. He played the final 23 games with the Hawks and performed well at both ends of the floor.

Coach Richie Guerin had come to the Hawks from the New York Knicks late in the 1964 season, became player-coach the next year and had remained ever since. As mod-looking as any of his players, Guerin wore a multi-colored sports coats and bell bottoms. But when he was working, he had the manners of a truckdriver. As a player, Guerin became the first guard in league history to score 2,000 points in a season, hitting 2,303 for a 29.5 average in 1962. He became a fulltime coach in 1967, but emerged from retirement to play in 27 games the next year. Toward the end of the 1969-70 season, he put on the playing togs when injuries to his team required it.

In the final game of the playoffs, Guerin did a remarkable thing. At age 37, he ran the team from the floor instead of the bench. When the Hawks didn't do what he wanted, he did it himself, driving at the Los Angeles Laker defense, stopping for his quick pop that was never quite a jump shot. In the end, the coach scored 31 points, desperately trying to keep his team in contention. But the Lakers won anyhow and went on to sweep the series. Guerin's effort alone reveals the nature of the man.

But his job with Maravich coming to the Hawks was bound to be his toughest ever. The world was changing and the sports scene was not excluded. Even on the college level Press Maravich saw it. "If I had to start all over again," he said, "I'd never coach with an assistant. I'd hire a psychiatrist. He'd be my assistant. I sure could use him to work on the complex emotions of today's kids."

The pro coach was often a casualty in the squabbles that arose within a team. Nice guys—the Dick McGuires, Johnny Kerrs—didn't last long. A man was either tough or he was out. But one N.B.A. coach was so hard on his players that at the end of the season they voted him out of a share of playoff money. It forced the league to rewrite the rules governing those spoils.

It seemed that Richie Guerin's former troubles would

be nothing stacked against what he could expect now. It would take a deft touch to keep harmony on the Hawks.

While Pete was waiting to join the Hawks, he was enjoying what seemed an endless summer. It was a respite from years of sweat and toil.

"I traveled nearly 14,000 miles one summer," he said, recalling pervious summers. "I worked mostly with kids in the seven-to-twelve age group. Kids older than that, say thirteen, fourteen, fifteen, are already interested in other things, like smoking cigarettes. They think they know it all. Athletics are out. They're more interested in being hippies and yippies, going off across the country, eating and sleeping wherever they can. A life like that doesn't do anything for me. I'd rather make a living for myself.

"I feel that by the time a guy gets to the seventh or eighth grade he should know what he wants to do in life. Then he should start working his butt off to become a success at it. You'll never find me at one of these rock festivals with a hundred thousand other people, sitting around with no shirt, drinking beer, and strumming on a guitar. You can't do that the rest of your life and you're fooling yourself if you think you can. There just isn't that much time on this earth. My way of expressing myself is through basketball. I've been at it a long time and I'm going to keep at it."

It was not a philosophy that suited a lot of young men of his age, but it paid off. The Pistol had his pick of product endorsements now. But Papa Press kept close tabs on the kind of exposure his son was offered. "Everyone wanted to stick Pete's name on everything,"

Press said. "We made it a rule that they had to come to me. No sense having all those guys bother Pete."

With Press screening the offers, some turned out to be quite profitable. Most were rejected outright. One was a legitimate movie offer, made even before Pete's excursion into the world of television. The Pistol was offered the title role in the film, *Drive, He Said*. The film dealt with a portion of the life of a college basketball star, his battle with traditional and radical values, both of which seem to offer an attraction to Pete. *Drive, He Said* was a first rate movie property. But Pete turned it down, saying he wasn't interested in portraying a college basketball player "who hits the skids. The guy even rapes a girl," he said. "That would have been real nice for my image."

Pete's image was elusive. He was guarded about his private life. Any discussion that verged on it he avoided. He refused to go beyond basketball in an interview. "The only part of my life I feel is still mine is my private life," he said. And he stuck to it. Despite the pressure of the media, he managed to take a goodly number of interviews. A conspicuous exception was *Women's Wear Daily*. The Pistol balked when he found the fashion paper planned to ask about his personal tastes in clothes, girls and furniture.

When an interviewer did occasionally probe, Pete chose his words carefully—like the time he talked to a pretty woman reporter for the *Atlanta Journal-Constitution*. It went something like this:

> Q: Is it true that you're not too fond of girls?
> PISTOL: Oh, no. I like the fairer sex as much as the next guy.
> Q: Have you ever thought about marriage?

PISTOL: Yes, I have. But my wife won't be living off the fat of the land. I guess my wants are like those of any other normal guy.

Q: Would she have to be a college graduate?

PISTOL: No, I don't think that it's so necessary for women to go to college. As a matter of fact, I saw the Secretary of Commerce on television the other day and he said he didn't graduate.

Q: Do you like kids?

PISTOL: Yes I do, especially when they're between six and twelve. That's when they listen, learn, and do what you tell them. When they get older, they're too interested in girls, cars, and that kind of stuff to learn well. But I really get involved with the younger ones when I'm teaching them basketball. Sometimes I have an urge to take them home. They're that good.

Q: What about the women's lib people playing basketball?

PISTOL: Great! We'd love it. The refs would sure keep busy. There'd be plenty of body contact.

In Atlanta, Pete rented a two-bedroom, townhouse apartment for $280 a month. Unlike the pretentious quarters of many big-bonus athletes, Pete's pad was modest. He allowed himself the luxury of a pool table and a seven-seat bar. Only a chamber maid, cat burglar, or very special friend could see the other frills—sheets, towels, bed spreads, shower curtains, dishes, glasses and even soaps containing the monogram "Pistol." It was something Pete said he'd dreamed of since acquiring the nickname as a youngster.

He also traded in his trusty old Volkswagen for a new Plymouth GTX with an engine that qualifies the car for competition at Atlanta International Speedway. Cradled under the dashboard was, of all things, a telephone. No one really knew why it was there, unless the Pistol placed mobile calls to his steady girlfriend of three years, whose identity he kept secret—"for her own sake," he said.

Atlanta was no different from other cities. Pete was recognized wherever he went. Unable to eat in public or see a movie, he ended up staying indoors. He kept to himself and to his apartment, in the company of a few friends. Like it or not he was in the spotlight. From the first moment he stepped onto the court in Atlanta, he was the man of the hour. And he had some mighty long hours ahead of him.

In time the pressure came. As rookie camp approached, the first wave of publicity hit. It was often fatuous. One writer figured Pete would have to play because of his contract. The thinking was that Guerin would rest all the regulars but Bellamy for eight minutes each. That way, Pete would get 32 minutes of playing time every game.

Pete's defense was thought to be bad. But Press disagreed. "Pete could always play defense," he said. "I've never doubted it for a minute. He's got the animal instincts, all of them—the quick hands, fast feet and a brain that reacts to basketball situations automatically, whether it be offense or defense."

Pete put it more simply. "It's nothing but hard work and guts, and I plan plenty of that," he said.

He meant it. Basketball is Pete's whole life. He thinks about it the way a doctor thinks about medicine or a lawyer about law. He has his own ideas about the game and where he stands in it. He told Noah Sanders prior to his rookie season:

"In the pros I won't be relied upon to always bring the ball downcourt. This leaves me great avenues. In the pros the man without the ball is always moving.

These men are geniuses. They have a sixth or seventh sense—if I come dribbling toward one of them, he already has a sense of all the things that can happen. It's something like a wavelength. They know and I know.

"Yeah, Bob Cousy had a lot of trouble getting people to accept his passes when he broke in. But that was back in the fifties, when you had the set shot and the basic chest pass. A very dull game. In the sixties, it was just about the same. But this is the seventies, and there are so many avenues. There are going to be 7-foot-4 centers—I mean common on each team—and they'll get faster. Before long the behind-the-back dribble will be a common thing.

"It's the most exciting sport in the world. There's always movement. If a guy's really knowledgeable in the game he can really freak out on it, if you want to say that. You see the different picks developing—man, look at that guy picking that guy and he don't really know it. And if something happens to go behind my back or through my legs—some fans enjoy that. They don't understand the game, but maybe that will win them over. You've got to have people in the stands. I'm just trying to help the game out. And there are so many avenues."

In Atlanta's rookie camp, Maravich got his first chance to do what he said he would. At the Westminster School in Atlanta, he gave the team officials their first look at him. In scrimmages against people like Bob Christian, Herb White, John Vallely, Bob Riley—all rookies—he was in the thick of the action, speeding into crowds, spinning away and firing incredible shots.

He came into the camp the quickest gun in town. He

was the guy all the others wanted to make their reputation against. "Yeah, it's rough," Pete conceded, "but the roughness is good. It's as it should be."

Even an ankle sprain he'd suffered just before camp began was no extenuating circumstance for Maravich. He knew that the pros played with hurts that would immobilize mere mortals. He had played that way before and didn't intend to change now.

The sight of Maravich with a slight crimp in his ankle inspired swarming tactics in the eager rookies, the kind that had gotten to him in the past. "Just before camp," Pete recalled, "I had the ball during a scrimmage in North Carolina. Suddenly I'm triple-teamed, with these guys clawing and reaching all over me. It just gets to a point . . . I threw the ball straight up in the air and walked off the court."

In the pros, he didn't have that privilege. The rough stuff was part of the game. And he fought fire with fire, battling through picks, diving for loose balls and, in the process, surprising observers who'd expected him to play with the arrogance of money. "The kid played more defense in two hours than he did in three years of college," said one reporter.

It was not the only surprise in that camp. On the last day at Westminster, several Hawk veterans appeared, drawn there no doubt to see what it's be like to play with and against Maravich. Pete gave them an eyeful, as he and Hazzard took turns turning it on. And before long, it seemed like prime time in the schoolyard, each player putting on a move that required topping. Round and round it went, and when it was over Maravich had made believers of the Atlanta people.

And yet Pistol knew it was only a beginning. He

thought of his game as an art that could grow if he let it. "I'm looking to pro ball," he said, "as a kind of graduate school where I hope to refine my talents. I don't think there'll be as much pressure on me in that there's no zone defense to worry about. But I'll have to find new ways of getting the ball to the open man. Guys like Walt Frazier don't get fooled more than once on the same play.

"I think John Havlicek is a perfect example of this type of thing. When he became a pro, he found talents he never knew existed. He didn't really have a chance, playing second fiddle to Jerry Lucas at Ohio State. But with the Celtics he matured as a ballhandler, dribbler, and playmaker. As for myself, I can't help but get better."

The next time he played with the pros that summer was at—of all places—a Catskills Mountain resort where bingo and "Simon Says" were the popular entertainments. Kutsher's Country Club was the last place one would expect to find the likes of Willis Reed, Wes Unseld, Dave Bing, Connie Hawkins, Billy Cunningham or Cazzie Russell. But every year the best of the pros wound up at the resort for the Maurice Stokes Memorial benefit game, played in honor of the late Cincinnati forward who was hospitalized for almost a decade before his death. First organized by Stokes' teammate and legal guardian Jack Twyman, the game brought the best pros around. Maravich didn't dare miss the chance.

And if he didn't have the stature of others there, he was, clearly enough, still the people's choice. That much became apparent when 2,000 people gathered for a demonstration originally scheduled for a few hundred. Pete regaled them with the Pretzel, the Banana, the Ricochet, the Bullet Ricochet, the TV Drill, the Machine Gun, and a few others. In this outlying area of basketball-crazy New York, he had the mob howling, right on down to the girl counselors from the local camps. In short order, Pete was the toast of the town.

The benefit appearance didn't allow him a moment's leisure. While seated at the dinner table with publicist Haskett Cohen, Pete was approached for an autograph by a pretty and noticeably nervous young girl. Cohen waved her off. But Pete insisted on signing. "No," he said. "I'm finished eating." Grabbing the pen, he wrote *Pistol Pete*.

"You'll make me a hero to my little brother," the girl crooned.

Pete just smiled.

Later that night on the arc-lit macadam court, after the stars had been divided into two teams, Maravich made his mark, too. With Dave Cowens of Florida State, first draft choice of the Boston Celtics, he injected some midwinter madness into the serene mountain night. He was not the uncanny shotmaker he'd been at L.S.U., but he passed the ball with the telepathic genius he'd developed as a collegian.

One time he moved down the lane, hard to his left. Suddenly, without blinking an eye, his arm shot out in the other direction, the ball spinning off swiftly to the open Cowens, who laid it in for the basket.

Minutes later, it was Pistol again, this time going the other way and whipping a behind-the-back pass to Cowens for a short jumper. He had his club moving. Seven times in the period, he penetrated the defense and slipped the ball to the open man. When it was over he had just 10 points. But his 12 assists and five or six steals aided his team's 86-82 victory.

"This was really my first taste of competition since the N.I.T. last March," he said afterward. "I know I didn't shoot well, but that doesn't bother me. It will come. I was very pleased with my defense. You don't get to steal the ball from guys like this every day."

Now the season closed in. Regular-season training camp was in Jacksonville, Florida. It was a time of high hopes and great expectations for N.B.A. rookies. For Pete Maravich, there was more pressure. He'd make the team, all right. With a million-dollar contract he had to. But he'd pay his dues for sure. "They've been saying they're gonna get him," an N.B.A. player said. "Some of those Hawk rookies, guys who were drafted lower than he was. And the veterans, too. I heard one say that while Pete is working on his moves, they're gonna be workin' on his head."

It didn't turn out that way. Other rookies got pounded, not Pete. "It looked like the word was out," said one reporter. "You know, hands off the merchandise. Can't lose this guy to a training camp injury." Another disagreed. "Pete's not getting hit," he said, "because the veterans respect him."

Captain Bridges had his own explanation. After several hard workouts, he was asked about Maravich avoiding the rough treatment. "He just seems to have a knack for working around and through the action," he said. "He handles a challenge with more finesse than anyone I ever saw. His quickness is so amazing that he often completely avoids physical contacts. And not because he's afraid. No, it's just that his talent is head and shoulders above any other rookie in camp. It flabbergasts me.

"To tell you the truth, right now I believe he will step on the court in our first game and play like someone who's been in the league for five years. Sometimes in practice I get the feeling that he's holding back some of his talents because he doesn't want to look too good yet."

If Maravich was not all there, Joe Caldwell was not there at all. "Pogo Joe," coming off the best season of his career, hadn't signed a contract. At first it seemed to be a routine holdout that players pull on managements that have lavished money on rookie prospects. It wasn't. Caldwell, it turned out, was fuming about the money that Maravich had gotten. He said he wouldn't sign with the Hawks unless they paid him "one dollar more" than the Pistol.

It became infectious. Pretty soon Bridges was squawking, too. "I don't think the Hawk management recognized my value as a ballplayer," he told reporters. "Not from the standpoint of what they're paying Maravich and Bellamy."

The whole world knew about Pete's contract and Big Bells was reputedly playing at the $80,000 level. Bridges was trying to renegotiate his four-year contract calling for $50,000 per. "Let me ask you something," the captain said. "Who was fourth in the league in rebounds last year? And who had the most playing time on the club? And who's been around here the longest? And who has to be the policeman on the court? I'll tell you who—Bill Bridges. I'm not asking for a million dollars, but I do expect to be compensated for my overall value to the Hawks."

In Bridges and Caldwell was reflected the dissatisfaction the team felt for Maravich. That he was not responsible for the circumstances of the market place didn't matter at all to them. Bridges and the others resented what they felt was the "special treatment" Maravich was accorded, a sentiment the captain made clear to Guerin in a private session with the coach. Bridges contended Pete got more instruction than the other rookies did.

Guerin disagreed emphatically. He suspended Bridges from the team for a short time—three or four hours at most. When tempers calmed, he restored Bridges to the captaincy of the team.

It did not augur well for Maravich and his teammates over an entire season. And Pete did little to quell the discontent in the exhibition games. With Atlanta he did not have the court to roam that he did at L.S.U. The other Hawks were not about to vacate their pieces of the floor to the rookie. Besides, it wasn't the way Atlanta played. Guerin's club used all its men, seeking out matchups and exploiting them.

Now when Pete drove he often ended up in the corners of the court where foes could double him and make it hard to get off a proper pass. When he did elude his defender and slip the quick pass off to a teammate, often the man was not ready for it. Maravich had a tempo of his own, and it took a while to get used to it.

He even lost his rhythm on the court. "I don't know what my problem is," Maravich said. "I can't seem to get in the groove out there. I'm not moving as well as I know I can and I'm disappointed. It's funny, but I'm almost too relaxed out there and I don't feel in good shape. A couple of days ago I thought I was ready."

It got worse and worse in the exhibitions. Turnovers came like tears before onions. In one game the Hawks lost the ball 46 times, three times the number that coaches condone. Maravich was getting his fair share of them, and Guerin was soon wagging his finger at him from the bench.

"He's getting wrapped up in the air with the ball," Guerin said. "In other words, when he slides off a pick, he's automatically going up for his shot. If you keep doing this in the pros, your opponent sees it and is just waiting to take the ball away. And Pete hasn't learned to mix a fake in there every once in a while to keep things honest."

In spite of the problems the public was hailing Maravich as the greatest thing for the game since Dr. Naismith. Wherever the team went the commotion was about the Pistol. It aggravated the other Hawks no end. "This team has a lot of pride," Guerin said. "We never place the individual above the team. But here it's being done for us. And a certain amount of resentment's appeared."

The Atlanta front office was as guilty as anybody. It billed the team as the "New Hawks" and created new insignia and uniforms. The veterans thought it degrading. It snubbed what they'd done in past seasons.

The discord peaked in the team's final exhibition contest against the Milwaukee Bucks in Nashville. The season was a week away and Atlanta was to open against the same Bucks on national TV. The afternoon of the exhibition the team loafed in their motel rooms, most of the players watching a football game.

At every commercial break came a reminder that a week from that day the nation would have the privilege of watching the professional debut of Pete Maravich. The regular season game was billed as Maravich against Alcindor, Oscar Robertson and the powerful Milwaukee Bucks. It was bound to give the Hawks an identity crisis.

It looked as though Atlanta was suffering from one that night in the preseason. They lost by 50 points with a nonchalance that prompted one Atlanta writer to say, "It was the worst exhibition of basketball I've ever seen. As far as I was concerned it was open rebellion."

Maravich was not insensitive to the sentiments of his teammates. "Sure," he said, "there are some petty jealousies around the league. Some people are bitter about what I got. But this is a business."

All the while he tried to bridge the gap. It wasn't easy. "Pete was desperately trying to make friends," said an observer. "Whenever he saw a group of players having a few drinks or something to eat he'd go over and join them and then insist on picking up the tab. All this did was serve to aggravate the situation. I'm sure Pete didn't realize it, but he was unconsciously rubbing it in, letting them know just who had all the money."

Joe Caldwell knew. Reportedly earning $60,000 a year before Maravich arrived, he was still demanding one dollar more than Pistol was getting. The final Hawk offer was a five-year pact starting at $110,000 and jumping by $10,000 each year until it reached $150,000. Joe said no and commenced negotiations with the A.B.A.

The advent of Maravich affected Hazzard, too. Though rated one of the better guards in the league,

Walt had had a nomadic career, playing originally with the Lakers before moving to the Supersonics, then to the Hawks. He suspected the worst now that Maravich was here. "Walt was uneasy right from the first," said Hawk Publicity Director Tom McCollister. "I remember asking him to pose for some publicity shots during the pre-season and he got really uptight about it. 'Whaddaya got me here for,' he said to me. 'I'm on my way out anyway.' And I understand he made similar statements all around the league. Like in each town he visited he'd look around and say, 'I wonder if I'll be a Hawk the next time I come here.' He was really bugged about it."

Bellamy was another problem and his situation was a little stranger than anyone else's. As one reporter told it, "Bellamy had a great pre-season. He was the only vet who looked good. He worked his tail off and seemed completely uninvolved with the Maravich thing. I guess it was because he was coming off his first title and it inspired him. But as soon as it was pretty certain that Caldwell wouldn't be back, Bells changed. It was as if he figured there was no chance now. He didn't play worthwhile ball again until February."

While Guerin publicly stated that he was happy about the Maravich draft, he had anticipated problems. Before the Hawks had chosen Pete, team owner Tom Cousins had asked Guerin, "What do you think about Maravich?"

Guerin answered, "No guard ever won an N.B.A. championship."

In fairness to the Hawk coach though, it should be said that once Pete came Guerin gave him all the help he could, knowing first-hand how hard it was to adjust to the pro game as a guard. "No doubt about it," he said, "there's no tougher position for a rookie to break in. The number of responsibilities are far greater than for those up front."

There was no escaping the reality of it all. It was not an easy spot to be in. "I don't envy Pete Maravich," one basketball man said. "He's going to have to earn those two million bucks."

At that price Pete was the sport's highest-paid benchwarmer when the regular season started. In Atlanta's opener against Milwaukee Maravich was not, as the TV network trumpeted, singlehandedly engaging the mighty Bucks in a game of baskets. At the opening tap he was not even on the court.

Guerin was not intending to rush him into battle prematurely in spite of the expectations of the world. For one thing, it was insulting to the Hawk veterans who had proved their mettle before. For another, Maravich needed to be handled with care. He had not yet learned what the pro game was all about.

"Pete has got to discipline himself to the obligations of a guard," said Guerin. "He's got a responsibility in that position to do the things I want him to do. He can't just dribble around. He's got to work plays. Contrary to what some people believe, I'm not trying to change Pete. I'm just trying to get him to use his talents in the right way. A lot of times the other guys have trouble following him."

Maravich chafed at being on the bench. All the great ones do. What made it more aggravating was that once the game started, he was still the attraction. Most of the photographers assigned to shoot the game stationed themselves by the Hawk bench to get candid shots of

The rookie's life isn't easy. Pete found this out quickly and took plenty of lessons from Atlanta Coach Richie Guerin before the season was over. "He made me see what it was all about," confessed the Pistol.

AL SATTERWHITE—CAMERA 5

On the court it was the opposition who did the teaching. Here Pete is hard-pressed to get by Warriors Jerry Lucas (32) and Jeff Mullins.

CHRIS SPRINGMAN—CAMERA 5

the Pistol on the wood. "I knew it would be hard for Pete to be on the bench," Guerin said, "but he never complained. Any player likes to start, especially one who's been the focal point of everything since the time he began playing ball."

On the court, the Hawks got along without him. Now that it was for real, Atlanta gave the appearance of being the sort of smooth-running outfit it had been in past seasons, and not the imprecise team it was in the exhibition campaign. The team jumped out to a six-point lead over Milwaukee in the first quarter.

Then, in the second quarter, Maravich got his chance. It was what the Atlanta crowd was waiting for. When he came onto the floor the cheers came from the highest rung of seats on down to courtside. It was what the people had come for.

It was not an easy way to break into the big-time. Even the Pistol was awed by it all. He moved about the court with uncertainty, and couldn't get into the flow of the game. From the bench, Guerin barked instructions—"Over! Over, Pete! . . . Come in now . . . come in! Back, now go back. For God's sake, go back!" One time Pete went the wrong way and collided with Hudson.

But the Hawks upped the lead while he was in the lineup, and were ahead by as many as 16 points. Gradually, Pete found his way. On a Milwaukee fast break, he dropped back quickly on defense, watching for the ballhandler to cue his pass. He guessed right and intercepted the ball. Pushing it out front of him, he drove downcourt. Just behind the foul line he skidded to a halt and sprang into the air. At the top of his leap he let the shot fly, a soft arching jumper. It went in and the Atlanta crowd erupted. Maravich had scored his first basket as a pro.

It was a memorable moment for Hawk backers that day. For suddenly the Bucks came on. Alcindor controlled the backboards and finally got his team running. On offense, Oscar Robertson began hitting his teammates—Greg Smith, Bob Dandridge, Jon McGlocklin—as they filled the lanes.

On defense, Alcindor became tigerish, taking the edge off the Atlanta attack. The shots the Hawks had cast without thought earlier they now thought about, a costly hesitation. Maravich added to the problems. He was not playing the game Guerin wanted. Too often he was going thoughtlessly to the corners of the floor, where he got into trouble. Midway through the third quarter, Pete got trapped in a corner and tried a cross-court pass. It got picked off by Dandridge who dribbled the length of the court for the "crip," an uncontested layup. Things went downhill quickly. At the end it was Milwaukee 107, Atlanta 98.

Maravich played 22 minutes and hit only three of 13 shots from the floor. He ended with seven points and a case of the blahs. After the game he refused to talk to reporters. He sat in a corner of the dressing room, arms folded, head down, stone still. When all the reporters but two had drifted from the room, he said, "What I played is called bad ball. I was ready physically. I've been playing better for a few weeks. But I wasn't there emotionally. After my first shot I was totally flushed. I felt like a ghost was sitting on top of me."

At the other end of the hallway, Milwaukee coach Larry Costello said, "He has to slow his tempo down. You can see that he's quick and handles the ball real well, but he'll have to make adjustments, and that's not going to happen overnight."

Costello was right. In the next weeks Pete suffered the usual rookie torments. It was as though the game was being played in another time zone. He was continually out of synch with his mates, hurtling downcourt with great sound and fury but doing pathetically little.

What made it worse was what Joe Caldwell did. He flew the Hawks' coop. He listened to what the Carolina Cougars' Jim Gardner offered and signed an A.B.A. contract. It was an irreparable loss for Atlanta, and the Hawks groused about the "Jonah" that Maravich was becoming. Pete was being blamed for Caldwell's defection.

When Caldwell left the Hawks lost the delicate balance that the best of teams have. He had served them the way Bill Bradley does the Knicks. He brought the best out in everybody. If Bradley does it with a subtle genius for passing, Caldwell did it with the flash and fire of his aggressive game. Maravich could not possibly restore what Caldwell gave Atlanta at this stage of his career.

That much was apparent to everybody who saw the Hawks play. In a game against Philadelphia, Maravich had the ball stolen from him. He dove in desperation for it and, as he tried to regain his feet, a courtside fan shouted, "Give Caldwell his money!"

It was of course too late.

After 16 games, things looked bleak: four wins and 12 losses. Guerin conceded that the loss of Caldwell had hurt the team, particularly on defense.

The situation was no better on offense. Theoretically, Hazzard was running the club, but as one Hawk said,

"Walt has to have the ball and Pete just wasn't willing to let him have it enough."

Guerin couldn't avoid the issue any longer. He admitted publicly that he had called his club together on two separate occasions during the pre-season to explain his handling of his high-priced rookie.

"One time some of our veterans said it looked like I was letting Maravich get away with more than the others," Guerin said. "To a degree, I was. I told them I had to learn about him. They all knew about my discipline, but I wanted to learn as much about his faults as I could. Even if it sometimes meant bending the rules a bit.

"Then there was a general resentment about his salary and all the publicity he was getting around the league. It was as if we'd never won the Western title the year before. I had to tell them it wasn't the kid's fault. But I understood how they felt, too. Everyone I met had the same question: 'How's Maravich doing?' It became tough on the other guys. And they were expecting help from him right away. I heard more than one guy say, 'Sure, we understand him getting all that money, but he has to do something for it.'"

One of Pistol's problems was that he was playing the way he had at Louisiana State. He was still trying to be a one-man band. He wouldn't pass the ball to Hazzard to start a set play. Often he just dribbled around waiting for something to happen. What happened more often than not was a turnover. And if his fancy passes went astray, the Hawks bristled even more. Showtime was a luxury they couldn't afford.

Pete continued to wind up in the corners of the floor. And the foe continued trapping him there. "By the time this happened," an Atlanta newsman said, "there'd be only about five or six seconds left on the 24-second clock and the Hawks were in trouble. Pete would look wildly about, trying to find a man. If he didn't throw the ball away, the guy that got it had about three seconds to shoot. There was no time to work any kind of set play."

Clearly, Pistol wasn't taking up Caldwell's slack. The other Hawks remained cool to him. He became increasingly the loner. And whatever he did it seemed to provoke the Hawks.

When the team went to Chicago, Pete and rookie Herb White got off the plane and out of the airport ahead of the others. Arriving at the hotel, they found two single rooms and the rest doubles. They took—what else?—the single rooms and left. When the other Hawks arrived and discovered their lodgings, it was not cordially received. Bridges ranted about the nerve of the rookies.

Soon after, Pete had to leave the team to film a commercial in Jacksonville. It did not go over big with the veterans that their millionaire backcourtman was off picking up some change. The problems were mounting.

Another time, a television crew arrived in Atlanta to prepare a documentary on the problems of a high-priced rookie. They arranged with the Hawk publicity department to speak with the Pistol and also Hudson, Hazzard and Bridges. "The other Hawks made their position quite obvious," says Al Silverman, editor of *Sport* magazine and the man in charge of the filming. "They were boycotting the interview. The three of them just sat there and wouldn't come out of the office. They'd had enough questions about Pete."

The Pistol cooperated and the film was made. But the Hawk front office apologized for an embarrassing situation. Not Guerin, though. He, too, was tired of Pete's ink. The whole affair upset him greatly and he was happy to see the film makers depart.

In Philadelphia, as the Hawks staggered around trying to catch the slick 76ers, a large banner was unfurled in the balcony of the Spectrum. It read: "HEY, PISTOL PETE, WHY DO HOT DOGS COST TWO MILLION DOLLARS IN ATLANTA AND ONLY 35 CENTS IN PHILADELPHIA?" When it rains, it pours.

The season was 13 games old when Pete earned his first start. He'd just come off a 23-point effort against the Detroit Pistons and Guerin felt it was time. Now Pete began to score. He started hitting from the outside and negotiating the driving lanes. He had games of 23, 28, 32, 32, 32 points. He was scoring big when the Hawks faced the defending champion Knicks in New York City.

The Knick fans are a rare breed. A couple of years before, Knick reserves Mike Riordan and Don May had come out early for some extra warm-up time. As they played a game of one-on-one, there were maybe two or three hundred fans in the arena. May had scored seven baskets before Riordan came back with six. As May got the ball again, a voice came bellowing down from above. "Come on, May, you're only up one basket!" Only at the Garden.

At the outset the Knicks moved in front. Guards Frazier, Barnett and Riordan were having an easy time. Again the Hawks looked dispirited. At one point, Pete

Even when he started, Pete had the omnipresent Guerin to contend with. A fiery leader and patient coach, Guerin and the Hawks rode out a horrendous start to drive into the playoffs. By then, Pete was an integral part of the team, sitting with veterans Lou Hudson (left) and Walt Bellamy during a time out.

CHRIS SPRINGMAN—CAMERA 5

got the ball on a fast break. He had Hazzard and Hudson flanking him. Instead of passing to the cutting Hazzard, he stopped and took a jumper from the key. At the next time out he went up to Hazzard and spoke with him. "I told him I realized he should have gotten the ball," Pete said later. "But I was afraid of Frazier coming up from behind. Even though I made the shot, it was still a bad play."

In the middle of the third period Pete began making good plays. The Knicks led by 20 at the time, but then Pete went to work. He faked, faked again and sped by Frazier for the basket. Next time down Frazier gave him more room. This time he drove right at him, stopped and arced a 20-footer. Next time it was a jumper from the side, then another twisting drive past Willis Reed. The Pistol was cranking up and the Garden fans were with him, coming to life and cheering every time he got the ball. Responding to the urgings of the sellout crowd, the Pistol kept it up. For one of the first times all year he had his confidence. The ball was his. The court was his. The game was his.

Late in the game he picked up a loose ball near the basket and without a second thought tossed in a 10-foot hook shot. The Garden erupted. Even the Hawk bench went wild. Fists shot into the air and a trace of a smile came over Guerin's face. The Pistol scored 14 of his team's next 24 points and 18 of their final 31. It wasn't enough to pull the game out, but his 40-point effort was a professional high. He was beginning to look like the real thing—on offense at least.

His defense was still weak, however, and Frazier had had a field day, scoring 33 points. "He's still learning the 'D'," Clyde said later. "He gives you a lot of room

"He's still learning the 'D'," said New York Knicks guard Walt Frazier. "He gives you a lot of room and gets lackadaisical on defense. Sure, he had his hand in my face, but you can't give guards 20-foot shots"

KEN REGAN—CAMERA 5

It was a different story at the other end of the court. Pete's work there prompted Frazier to say, "He makes some unbelievable shots himself, don't he?"

UPI

and gets lackadaisical on defense. Sure, he had his hand in my face, but you can't give guards 20-foot shots. You've got to get up on them. But I'll say this, he makes some unbelievable shots himself, don't he?"

Indeed he did, and continued to, but it didn't resuscitate the Hawks. As November dragged to December and into the new year, Atlanta remained bogged down.

There were those who traced the trouble to Pete. He wasn't fitting in. One Atlanta newsman felt that the team had a defeatist complex, and it was all Pete's fault. The local press turned on him regularly, and for a three-week period in January he refused all interviews. "By now Pete's personality had changed," says a reporter. "He had given up trying to make friends with the other Hawks. It looked as if he'd become bitter and sullen. He wasn't happy."

But through it all the Maravich name was like old gold. He continued to be the most sought-after Hawk for autographs, speaking engagements and interviews. The man who attended to much of this was publicity director Tom McCollister. "We made Pete generally available to the public," McCollister says. "Except for a brief time when he refused all interviews, he got along very well with the media people. Of course, he still didn't like interviews that dealt with his personal life.

"There was a constant demand for Pete to make personal appearances. We have no general rule for that. I always try to get Pete to large gatherings, judging by importance and need. We like to bring him before kids. They really relate to him and he handles them very well. As for autographs, Pete usually signs, but he likes to sign all, or none. He won't sign for 50 kids, then say no to the next 50 who have been patiently waiting. I remember him standing in the rain in Cleveland earlier in the year and signing autographs for about 200 kids."

Several groups attempted to start Maravich fan clubs, but they rarely materialized. "Sometimes they'd say they had a fan club just to get Pete to come down," McCollister says. "There was one, however, that lasted throughout the season, *The Pete Maravich Fan Club of Cobb County,* with about 30 members ranging in age from nine to 17. Pete went down there several times, talking with the members, posing for pictures and handing out autographs. Pete and the boys got along great," says McCollister.

Pete increasingly kept to himself to avoid the constant attention he got in public. It led him to stay in his own apartment, where his unlisted phone number had to be changed twice. But that wasn't the only thing that changed.

When Pete first came to Atlanta dressed in a dark suit and vest to sign his contract, he was described as looking "like a banker." But in the debonair world of the N.B.A. he was persuaded to adopt a new look. On the team's first trip to New York, Guerin, Bridges and Hudson took the Pistol to a swank clothier that specialized in made-to-order apparel. Pete purchased six or seven mod suits and afterward admitted, "I only have about 20 suits and 15 pairs of shoes and boots now. But give me time. I just got here. Before long I should have triple that amount in clothes."

Later in the year he was considered for inclusion in a *Time* magazine article on the mod athlete as a leader in fashion. Some of those featured in the full-color, picture story were the dandyish Ken Harrelson, Walt Frazier, Derek Sanderson and Eddie Belmonte, all known for

The kids were always a big part of Pistol's life. When he signed one autograph, he signed them all, often lingering for more than an hour after a game to accommodate his rabid fans.

AL SATTERWHITE—CAMERA 5

their flamboyant and colorful life styles. *Time* contacted an Atlanta newsman and told him about the proposed story, asking if Pete would fit in. The writer had to be honest. Pete wasn't ready, he said. He'd have to wait till next year.

On the court Pete didn't want to wait till next week. The time to do it was now. He worked to get the economy of movement that Guerin advised. It wasn't easy. He still made mistakes that put off his teammates.

"He came here as an individualist," says Bridges. "There was plenty of sensationalism and an attraction for the fans. But we go on as teammates. We've been programmed to play as a team. I, for one, have never played this game as an individual and I never will. I'm a veteran and he's a rookie. Until he can perform with a certain knowledge and consistency, he's still a rookie. And there's no way I'll cater to a rookie. It's up to him to come into the group."

Maravich worked to win the respect of the team— and he did it at both ends of the court. When L.A.'s Jerry West scored 36 points against him, he declared that it wouldn't happen again. Guerin pointed out that former Hawk Don Ohl had once made a similar claim after West hit for 51. Ohl played his heart out the next time the two teams met and, by consensus, did a good job. Nonetheless, West got 52 points.

"I'll bet you five he doesn't get 36 again," Pete said to his coach.

"You're on," answered Guerin, later adding, "That'll be the sweetest five I ever lost."

"Jerry West is the best," said Pete at the time. "And you always want to be better than the best. It's a challenge to play him. And I'm ready to take that challenge and make the most of it." The next time Atlanta played Los Angeles, Pete met the challenge. He held West to 24 points.

In Philadelphia, things got hairier. On his way from the locker room to the court for pregame warmups, Pistol was accosted by a horde of young girls, "Peeeeete," they shrieked, "Peeeeeete." He'd take on Jerry West, but not these ladies. Maravich ran.

"They just wanted to muss your hair a little," teased a teammate later.

"Muss it! They wanted to pull it. And I've got plenty of hair to pull."

Back on the court he ran into the thick of things. He twisted, drove and jumped past the frustrated 76er defenders all night. In the fourth quarter he scored 18 points to lead the Hawks to a 130-125 victory.

The Hawks were moving up. The team still trailed Baltimore and Cincinnati in the Central Division and chances for a playoff berth looked dim. But for the first time all year the rhythm was there. It looked as though Atlanta could be a winner.

In late January the team traveled to Buffalo for a game with the expansion Braves. Earlier in the season the Hawks were beaten badly in that city. The Buffalo center, Bob Kauffman, had scored 34 points against Bellamy and had moved him about with ease.

This time the Hawks held a meeting. All the players but Maravich were there. From the meeting came this resolve: the Hawks decided to play with Pete and not against him. They started that night in Buffalo, winning 123 to 113.

Maravich, after averaging almost six turnovers a game, began to be flawless. "There's a good reason for this," said one team observer. "The other players were consciously helping him. If he did get trapped in a corner, there'd be movement among the other players. There'd be someone open, someone he could get the ball to. I really don't know who changed more, Pete or the other Hawks, but you could see the difference."

Pistol limited fancy passes, dribbled less and passed more. His shooting improved and down the stretch he was hitting better than 50 percent of his shots. The Hawks noticed this. "In the beginning Pete was very much withdrawn," says Bridges. "He was always by himself—in the dressing room, on the bus, in the airport. The Hawks are a team. Personally, I was not willing to accept him as an individual, only as a teammate. I think we've relaxed our resistance to him as an individual. In the dressing room now he's beginning to smile more. He's relaxed. He comes up to the other guys and starts talking. As a team, the big thing we're missing is Caldwell. We needed him in the corner. But I think we're all together again. We all know what we have to do. Pete, for instance, has the potential to be a great pro. We all know that. But he can't be controlling the ball on this team. Walt [Hazzard] has to. That way Pete can just filter in with the general flow of play. When he wasn't starting, he'd feel he had to show something quick and start controlling the ball. But with someone controlling him, he'll be better. And we'll win."

"Yes, I was frustrated at the beginning," Maravich admits. "Sometimes I couldn't see straight. It was that bad. And Richie kept it like that when he kept me on the bench. I never sat in my life. I was coming into games frozen stiff. But he finally brought it out of me.

He made me see what it's all about. He kept on me and kept on me. Sometimes until it seemed I'd go crazy.

"I can tell you one thing, though. It's because of him that I climbed over the hill out of the valley of disgust. He's handled me just right as far as I'm concerned. I remember about six games ago, when I was taken off the floor after a pretty good effort. The coach just reached over and patted me on the head. That did it. That tap meant everything in the world to me. I think his whole plan was beautiful. He brought me out and I'm just beginning to feel that everything is in place."

It needed to be for the Hawks to make up the ground they'd lost early in the year. Going into the final month, Atlanta was still behind Baltimore and Cincinnati in the Central Division. In that four-team conference only the top two teams would qualify for the prestigious playoffs that followed the regular-season schedule.

Since the All-Star break in January, an improved Maravich had given the Hawks the game that Guerin prescribed, a sort of controlled fury. Like Namath in pro football, Maravich had wheeler-dealer instincts that had to be curbed. And like Joe Willie, he'd gone through hell and high water to do it.

Slowly but surely, the frills went out of his game. Not that he abandoned the crowd-pleasing ballhandling. He simply learned when to turn it on. As Namath had to learn not to force the pass through crowds of defenders, Maravich had to learn to control his passes. It made him a more effective but no less exciting performer.

And it made the Hawks winners. From the All-Star break on, Atlanta began cutting Cincinnati's lead, winning 17 of 29 games. Cincinnati began faltering. On March 10, the Hawks played their best game of the year, drubbing the Phoenix Suns, 139-98. In that one, Maravich scored 37 points, had nine rebounds and stole five Pheonix passes.

"No doubt about it now," Guerin said. "Maravich is the rookie of the year. He's the best rookie in this league and I just don't see how anybody could vote otherwise."

But Guerin's was not the majority verdict. The Phoenix coach, Cotton Fitzsimmons, was one of the many who disagreed. "If I had the choice I'd vote for Dave Cowens," he said. "Maybe he hasn't scored as much, but he's been more consistent for the entire season and his team is a winner. The Celtics lost more than 40 games last year and are now 40-36. Cowens is the only new face. And the Hawks were division champs last year, a loser this year. Maravich is the only new face."

Others lauded Portland's Geoff Petrie, but Guerin was not sold on him to the extent he was on his own man. "When Petrie goes up for a shot," he said, "he seldom deviates. He rarely passes off. That leaves our guys set to go with him all the way. On the other hand, Pete hides his intentions."

One thing was for sure. Neither Cowens nor Petrie had to perform under the pressure that Maravich did. In Portland, Petrie could—and did—gun the ball when he wanted and nobody there griped. He was not under the intense scrutiny that Maravich was and had only the scoring column to worry about. The expansion Portland team, a first-year club, was not expected to win ball games.

The pressure was greater for Cowens, and he met it

The late-season Maravich was once again a driving, penetrating guard and an all-around offensive threat. Airborne against the Chicago Bulls, Pistol gets set to fire a mid-air pass that led to an Atlanta hoop.

UPI

Of John Havlicek, Pete said, "When he became a pro, he found talents he never knew existed." And playing against Havlicek, Pistol had to call on all of his extraordinary talents just to survive. It was part of a complete N.B.A. education.

AL SATTERWHITE—CAMERA 5

admirably. But it was not Maravich's burden. And in the end it was Pistol, not Petrie or Cowens, who helped get his team to the playoffs.

For the final weeks of the season, Maravich was the driving, slashing kind of performer he'd been at L.S.U., dribbling through defenses with the intuition he'd gained from years of work. Jump shot, hook shot, layups—he made them all. By the end of regular season play he'd emerged as the league's eighth best scorer with 1,880 points in 81 games, an average of 23.2 p.p.g. Of the Hawks, only Hudson scored more. The Pistol also finished with a .458 shooting percentage, higher than he'd ever had at L.S.U. He was an 80 percent shooter from the free throw line, and collected 298 rebounds and 355 assists. He fouled out of only one game.

They were superb figures, but not enough apparently for the selectors of the league's Rookie-of-the-Year. Petrie and Cowens tied for the honor. The Pistol was a distant third. "It's a disgrace that Pete Maravich was not named Rookie of the Year," said Guerin. "Cowens and Petrie are fine players, but neither had a rookie year like Pete, and mark my words, neither will accomplish what Pete will accomplish in this league. There wasn't a better rookie in this league than Pete. I put him in the same class as Oscar, West and Monroe, when they came up. You know, it's difficult for a man Pete's age to handle the constant pressure that he was exposed to all year. He always impressed me the way he kept his cool and through all the criticism and hostilities that he had to face. To do all that and still have a rookie year like he had, you gotta be some kind of ballplayer."

One who looked at it somewhat differently was an Atlanta newsman who covered the team all season long. He voted for Pete as the top rookie, but saw how others might not. But, he added, the out-of-town writers couldn't really appreciate what the Pistol had gone through.

"This kid really suffered, even at the end when things were going his way," the reporter said. "The team played a game in Cincinnati when they were still fighting for the playoff berth. The place was packed and Pete responded. He had 43 points and kept the Hawks in it almost singlehandedly. But at the same time Archibald [Nate Archibald, a Royals guard] had a phenomenal night, scoring 48. That loss stunned Pete. He was totally heartbroken. I really saw what kind of ballplayer he was that night."

He was hurt, too, by the vote of his peers. In a poll conducted by *The Sporting News* the players voted for Rookie of the Year and Cowens won. Even worse, Pete got just six votes and finished behind people like John Hummer and Calvin Murphy. He told Tom McCollister, "I'd like to find those six guys who voted for me and take them all out to dinner."

What consolation he got from the season came when the Hawks slipped into a playoff berth in the final days of the season. It was a long way from the dreary winter nights. April was not the cruelest month for the Hawks. It was playoff time.

There was money to be made in the playoffs. The winning team stood to earn $212,000 or $16,000 a man.

Beyond that was the glory. It meant more than money could buy to the men in the N.B.A.

It was a feverish time. The league allowed only the better officials to work the big games, indicating the stakes involved. The players performed with a fury seen infrequently in the 82-game regular season. Even the fans picked it up. The year before, in the Knicks' playoff drive to the league title, the New York gallery had often chanted profanely when it disagreed with referees' calls. The games had a force that the players seemed unable to control. It required a lot of self control to last out the playoffs.

The stress of these games was unbelievable, and it gave experienced teams an edge. In Madison Square Garden, where Atlanta was to play defending champion New York, the din could shatter the composure of veterans.

And yet for Maravich, it was his kind of magic. Throughout his basketball career he'd looked to nights like these. He thrived on entertainments. But like other great rookies before him, he felt the pressure. In New York, where the series opened, he did not have the derring-do he had earlier in the year there.

If he'd beaten Walt Frazier to the basket then, he did not now. Clyde, and the other Knicks, were playing as well as they had all year. With team captain Willis Reed injured most of the time, the Knicks had struggled in regular season. But now they got their game together.

Through the first four games of the series, Maravich was not the shooter he'd been at the end of the year. He led the Hawks in scoring in the first game with 23 points, but even then he was missing more than the team could afford. Only Bellamy, the "Dr. Strangeglove" of pivot play, performed with any consistency. It helped that Reed had tendonitis of the knees, but even that, he was hitting on some incredible shots. Bellamy's teammates were outplayed, plain and simple.

Only once did the Hawks manage to confuse the Knicks. In the second game of the series, Guerin inserted 6-9½ reserve, Jim Davis, at forward against the 6-5 Bill Bradley. Davis immediately moved into a low pivot against Bradley and down the stretch "burned" him with short-range jumpers.

It was a tactic that other teams had tried against New York. Sometimes it succeeded. But what it did was to force the ball to a man who was not the other team's best shooter. Frequently, it just disrupted the attack.

Although it worked in the second game of the series —Atlanta won—it never worked thereafter. Bradley solved the problem by "fronting" Davis, stationing his body between his man and the ball. Nimbler than Davis, he kept him from getting his hands on the ball.

It was no problem for Maravich to get the basketball. But neither he nor Hazzard in the backcourt could get the Hawks going. After four games, New York led, 3-1. The series moved from Atlanta to New York. A victory for the Knicks would eliminate the Hawks from the playoffs.

Back at the Garden the place was again sold out— 19,500 fans ranging from the Dustin Hoffmans' seated directly behind the Knicks' bench to the outrageous schoolkids up in the rafters who'd chant "Mendy is a bum." The reference was to official Mendy Rudolph, a swarthy and dandyish fellow who was the best known official in the league.

Pistol Pete Maravich in full stride as a standout performer with the Atlanta Hawks.

UPI

For Pete now, the dreams of an N.B.A. championship.
AL SATTERWHITE—CAMERA 5

In the Garden, the fans knew their personnel—from the players on down. They had that kind of maven's feeling for the game. That was why they could rise up and cheer when Maravich gave them the artistry he was capable of. He'd failed to do it in the first four games, but this night he became explosive.

After a first half in which Pete had scored 10 points to help the Hawks to a 57-53 lead, Guerin went to him and said, "Get back out there and drive." For an eight-minute stretch in the third quarter he did just that.

It was a sight to see. Against Frazier, whose hands were the quickest in the game, he juggled his rhythms to get the step he needed. Then, as the defense-minded Knicks rallied to Frazier's side, Maravich time and again eluded them in midair, slipping the ball by their outstretched fingertips for baskets. Or he'd stop quickly and go up for his jumpshot.

Suddenly he was running the game. In that eight-minute burst he hit eight of the ten shots he took, each more incredible than the last. The Knicks couldn't stop him. Not until the fourth quarter, that is. Maravich hit two shots at the outset that gave Atlanta an 89-80 lead. Then again he pounded to the hoop, running full force this time into big Reed. It was a bone-jarring collision. But Pete stayed in the game, only to be struck inadvertently by an elbow from Reed's replacement, seven-footer Greg Fillmore. It left him seeing double and Guerin was not willing to risk Pistol's guessing which hoop was the real one. He sat him down.

When Maravich returned several minutes later, he'd lost his edge. He missed his first four shots, one of them a layup. Meantime, the Knicks moved up, playing in the last five minutes, as one writer put it, like a group that didn't want to get off the court in a playground. When the game ended, Maravich had scored 31 points, but it was not enough to stop New York. The final: Knicks 111, Hawks 107.

It was a hard way for him to go out. But then it had been the toughest year of his life. "Pete came here as an idealistic young man," recalled team publicity director Tom McCollister. "There were certain things he just accepted as general truths. He wasn't ready for all the things that had to happen to him . . . and did."

It was not quite the blaze of glory with which Pete had hoped to finish the season, but it was a promise of things to come. He'd fought his battles and won his spurs. And now, as he sat dejectedly in a corner of the locker room, his teammates let it be known that Maravich was all right with them. Reserve player Jerry Chambers came over, patted his shoulder and said, "You played, man. Don't let anybody tell you that you didn't."

And nearby Walt Hazzard said what everybody knew.

"He is," said Hazzard, "going to be a monster."

It sounded like a warning.

Statistics

HIGH SCHOOL RECORDS

Daniels High (sophomore)
Most points scored: 483
Needham–Broughton (junior and senior)
Most points in a single season: 735
Most points in two seasons: 1,185
Best point average for a single season: 32 points per game in 23 games
Best point average for a single season 32 points per game in 46 games
Most times over twenty points in a game in a single season: 21
Most times over twenty points in a game in two seasons: 31
Most times over thirty points in a game in a single season: 11
Most times over thirty points in a game in two seasons: 13
Most times over forty points in two seasons: 6
Most times in double point figures for two seasons: 45

PETE'S COLLEGE RECORDS

NCAA
Highest points per game average (season): 44.5 (1969–70)
Highest points per game average (career): 44.2 (1967–70)
Most points scored (season): 1381 (1969–70)
Most points scored (career): 3667 (1967–70)
Most field goal attempts (season): 1168 (1969–70)
Most field goal attempts (career): 3166 (1967–70)
Most field goals made (season): 522 (1969–70)
Most field goals made (career): 1387 (1967–70)
Most free throw attempts (game): 31 vs. Oregon State, (12-22-69)
Most free throws made (game): 30 vs. Oregon State, (12-22-69)
Widest scoring margin in single season: 10.9— Maravich, 44.2; Mount, 33.3 (1968–69)

SOUTHEASTERN CONFERENCE

Conference Games
  Points scored: 69 vs. Alabama, 2-7-70
  Field goal attempts: 57 vs. Vanderbilt, 1-29-68 and 57 vs. Alabama, 2-7-70
  Field goals made: 26 vs. Vanderbilt, 12-11-69 and 26 vs. Alabama, 2-7-70
  Free throw attempts: 27 vs. Florida, 2-12-69
  Free throws made: 22 vs. Florida, 2-12-69

Conference Season
  Points scored: 851 (1969–70)

Pistol Pete

Average points: 47.3 (1969–70)
Field goal attempts: 741 (1969–70)
Field goals made: 336 (1969–70)
Free throw attempts: 243 (1967–68)
Free throw attempts (all games): 436 (1969–70)
Free throws made: 199 (1967–68)
Free throws made (all games): 337 (1969–70)

Conference Career
Points scored: 2383 (1967–70)
Field goal attempts: 2110 (1967–70)
Field goals made: 915 (1967–70)
Free throw attempts: 720 (1967–70)
Free throws made: 553 (1967–70)
Assists: 257 (1967–70)

LSU
Assists, single season: 192 (1969–70)
Assists, career: 425 (1967–70)

ALL-TIME COLLEGE SCORERS

		School	Years	Points
1.	**Pete Maravich**	LSU	**3**	**3667**
2.	Oscar Robertson	Cincinnati	3	2973
3.	Elvin Hayes	Houston	3	2884
4.	Rich Hamric	Wake Forest	4	2587
5.	Calvin Murphy	Niagara	3	2548
6.	Frank Selvy	Furman	3	2538
7.	Bill Bradley	Princeton	3	2503
8.	Elgin Baylor	Seattle	3	2500
9.	Tom Gola	LaSalle	4	2462
10.	George Dalton	John Carroll	4	2357

	School	Years	Points
11. Lew Alcindor	UCLA	3	2325
12. Rick Mount	Purdue	3	2323
13. Billy McGill	Utah	3	2321
14. Don Flora	Washington & Lee	4	2310
15. Jerry West	West Virginia	3	2309
16. Rick Barry	Miami	3	2298

ALL-TIME LSU SCORERS

	Yrs.	Seas.	Games	Pts.	Ave.
Pete Maravich, g	**1967-69**	**3**	**83**	**3,667**	**44.2**
Bob Pettit, f-c	1951-54	3	76	1,970	25.9
Roger Sigler, f	1953-57	4	77	1,338	17.4
Dick Maile, f	1963-65	3	74	1,274	17.2
Bob Meador, f	1947-51	4	99	1,163	11.7
Joe Dean, g	1949-52	3	69	1,072	15.5

COLLEGE VARSITY TOTALS

G	Min	FG	FGA	Pct.	FT	FTA	Pct.	RB	A	PF	TP	Ave.
83	***	1387	3166	.438	893	1152	.775	528	423	250	3667	44.2

FIRST YEAR N.B.A. TOTALS
(regular season)

81	2926	738	1613	.458	404	505	.800	298	355	238	1880	23.2

(Atlantic Division Semi-Finals)

5	199	46	122	.377	18	26	.692	26	24	14	110	22.0